get Messy!

BRF Ministries, 15 The Chambers, Vineyard, Abingdon OX14 3FE
+44 (0)1865 319700 | enquiries@brf.org.uk
brf.org.uk

The **Messy Church©** name and logo are registered trade marks of Bible Reading Fellowship, a charity (233280) and company limited by guarantee (301324), registered in England and Wales

ISBN 978 1 80039 287 8

First published 2024

All rights reserved

This edition © Bible Reading Fellowship 2024

Acknowledgements

Scripture quotations marked with the following abbreviations are taken from the version shown. Where no abbreviation is given, the quotation is taken from the same version as the headline reference. NIV: The Holy Bible, New International Version (Anglicised edition) copyright © 1979, 1984, 2011 by Biblica. Used by permission of Hodder & Stoughton Publishers, a Hachette UK company. All rights reserved. 'NIV' is a registered trademark of Biblica. UK trademark number 1448790. ERV: Copyright © 2006 by Bible League international. NIRV: Copyright © 1995, 1996, 1998, 2014 by Biblica, Inc.®. Used by permission. All rights reserved worldwide. NLV: the New Life Version, copyright © 1969 and 2003. Used by permission of Barbour Publishing, Inc., Uhrichsville, Ohio 44683. All rights reserved. CEB: Copyright © 2011 by Common English Bible. NRSV: the New Revised Standard Version Updated Edition. Copyright © 2021 National Council of Churches of Christ in the United States of America. Used by permission. All rights reserved worldwide. NLT: The Holy Bible, New Living Translation, copyright © 1996, 2004, 2007, 2013. Used by permission of Tyndale House Publishers, Inc., Carol Stream, Illinois 60188. All rights reserved.

Subeditor: Becca Turnbull

Designer: Ben Bloxham

Proofreader: Daniele Och

Cover photos: © BRF Ministries

Internal photos: © BRF Ministries. Activity photos © session writers.

Photocopying for churches

Please report to CLA Church Licence any photocopy you make from this publication. Your church administrator or secretary will know who manages your CLA Church Licence.

The information you need to provide to your CLA Church Licence administrator is as follows:
Title, Author, Publisher and ISBN.

If your church doesn't hold a CLA Church Licence, information about obtaining one can be found at **uk.ccli.com**.

Photocopying of any part of this magazine is otherwise not permitted. Additional print or digital copies can be purchased at brfonline.org.uk/getmessyvol2.

To order back issues of *Get Messy!* and other Messy Church resources, email BRF Ministries at **enquiries@brf.org.uk** or telephone **+44 (0)1865 319700**.

Send in news, stories, photos and general enquiries to our Messy Church administrator on **+44 (0)1235 858238** or **messychurch@brf.org.uk**.

What is Messy Church?

It's church, but not as you know it.

Every month thousands of people of all ages come together to discover Jesus, including those who've never been to church before. In over 30 countries around the world, we eat, play and worship together. Expect activities, songs and prayers and an entirely new way to express your faith.

Look out for the following symbols by activities, which give you extra materials and more!

PDF DOWNLOAD
This symbol means you can go to **messychurch.org.uk/getmessyvol2-2878** to download templates at A4 size, including a session planning sheet.

MESSY CHURCH AT HOME
Activities with this symbol can be used for 'take-home' ideas, to continue the God-conversation between Messy Church gatherings.

MESSY CHURCH GOES WILD
This symbol shows activities that work well for Messy Church Goes Wild sessions. See **messychurch.org.uk/goeswild** for more ideas.

contents

07 AIKE WRITES

08 SEPTEMBER
WHO IS GOD? WHAT IS GOD LIKE?

13 OCTOBER
WHO IS JESUS? IT'S ALL ABOUT LOVE

18 NOVEMBER
WHO IS JESUS? IT'S ALL ABOUT GRACE

23 DECEMBER
GOD ENTERS THE WORLD

28 JANUARY
'IT'S NOT FAIR!' IT'S ALL ABOUT MERCY

33 FEBRUARY
WHAT DID JESUS SAY? 'I FORGIVE YOU'

38 MARCH
ALL CAN BE SAVED

43 APRIL
JESUS CARES FOR US:
JESUS' LAST MEAL WITH HIS FRIENDS

49 MAY
IS GOD REAL? REMEMBER ME!

55 JUNE
WHO IS THE HOLY SPIRIT?

60 JULY
'COME, FOLLOW ME'

66 AUGUST
CAN I TRUST GOD? A NEW DIRECTION

Meet our session *Writers*

Karen Ashton is a volunteer Messy Church leader at Selly Oak Methodist Church and has been involved in Messy Church for over six years. Karen enjoys all forms of craft activities especially those that can be made by reusing or recycling.

Sandy Brodine is a younger generations education and strategy coordinator for the synod of Victoria and Tasmania in Australia. She has a passion for creative worship and for helping new disciples grow imaginatively and strongly in faith. She lives with her husband, daughter and two dogs in Mitcham, Victoria.

Jocelyn and Alex Czerwonka have recently retired to Whanganui in the north island of Aotearoa New Zealand. Both have been involved in Messy Church for many years and are members of the National Aotearoa New Zealand Messy Church team. Their favourite role is being granny and grandad to their five delightful grandchildren.

May Dappa is a volunteer leader at St Richard's Messy Church, Charlton, in south-east London. She enjoys working with children and young people, as well as taking care of her family.

Rachel Gotobed works within The Salvation Army's family ministries department. She is a passionate advocate for autism acceptance and inclusion, a cake baker, a script/song writer and loves writing for Messy Church and being part of the prayer team.

Lydia Harrison is team leader of the Messy Church prayer support team and a member of the writers support team. She also works as children and family work enabler for the Goole and Selby Methodist Circuit. She loves cows.

Deborah Humphries worked with adults and young people at **Great Barr Messy Church**, who are celebrating their tenth birthday this year. They usually get very messy during Messy Church and enjoy supporting one another through the mess of faith and life.

Arul Israel is a youth and children worker for the Birmingham Methodist Circuit. She loves working with young people and dancing Bharatanatyam (a classical Indian dance), including choreographing and performing liturgical dances as part of worship.

Becky May is founder of The Resources Cupboard, supporting the local church to make young disciples. She helps lead a Messy Church and enjoys engaging with Messy Church with her family. Becky is a member of the Messy Church writing and training teams.

Jillian Mayer is over the moon to be contributing to this edition of *Get Messy!* Over the past seven years, her love of Messy Church has continued to grow after witnessing firsthand the impact it has had on her church. She currently serves as the director of Christian education and faith formation at St Paul United Church of Christ in Waterloo, Illinois.

Johannah Myers is the associate director of Messy Church USA and, since 2013, has led a Messy Church at the church where she works as the director of disciple formation. She has a passion for intergenerational faith formation and all things Messy.

Anne Offler is based in County Durham and has worked with Sharon Pritchard and numerous Messy Churches for many years. Anne is a Methodist local preacher and writes resources for churches and children's ministry publications.

Formerly part of the Messy Church team at BRF Ministries, **Martyn Payne** has a background in teaching, Bible storytelling and leading all-age worship. He is pastor of a church in Essex, where he is in the early stages of establishing a monthly, mainly outdoor, Messy Church.

Sharon Pritchard is based in County Durham and works alongside Anne Offler and many Messy Churches. Sharon is children's ministry adviser for the diocese of Durham and writes resources for churches and children's ministry publications.

Greg Ross is a Uniting Church Minister and is one of the regional coordinators for Messy Church Western Australia. He is passionate about building up local congregations to collaborate with God on mission in each community, so everyone is welcome at church.

Sharon Sampson is a photographer, dog walker and mum of three from a little village in the English countryside. She loves showing all ages that being a Christian can be a fun adventure!

Karen Ashton

Sandy Brodine

Jocelyn and Alex Czerwonka

May Dappa

Rachel Gotobed

Lydia Harrison

Great Barr Messy Church

Arul Israel

Becky May

Jillian Mayer

Johannah Myers

Anne Offler

Martyn Payne

Sharon Pritchard

Greg Ross

Sharon Sampson

Messy Basics: A discipleship course

Exploring what Christians believe through faith-based conversations in all-age groups

Messy Basics complements the session material in *Get Messy! Volume 2* so that the same topic can be explored between Messy Church gatherings but using different Bible passages, or it can be used on its own. *Messy Basics* is a discipleship course comprising twelve sessions that are both an ideal way to introduce people to the basics of Christian faith but also to ground believers (whether just out of the starting blocks or seasoned sages) in the truths of the gospel. It works well for baptism preparation, family devotional time or any intergenerational group. Available as separate sessions or the full course.

PDF DOWNLOAD | £1.99 per session or £9.99 for full course | brfonline.org.uk

D♡nate to
Messy Church
BRF Ministries fundraising team

Our vital ministry supporting Messy Churches across the UK and the world would not be possible without your generous support. Through your donations we are able to offer training, resources, events and more to Messy Churches and their teams, helping people of all ages to encounter Jesus.

Making a donation to Messy Church really does make a huge difference. We are grateful to everyone who has made a donation and to all those who have signed up to become a Friend of Messy Church by making a regular donation of £2 a month or more. These donations make a lasting difference to our work, allowing us to plan for the future.

If you or your church would like to become a Friend of Messy Church, you can do so at **brf.org.uk/friends**.

You can also regularly raise money at no extra cost to yourself by using Give as you Live when you shop online or in some shops. Each purchase you make raises funds which go towards supporting and resourcing Messy Churches. You can find out more and sign up at **brf.org.uk/easy-ways-to-support-brf-at-no-cost-to-you**.

If you would like to make a difference to Messy Church by sponsoring a specific project, please do contact our fundraising team via **giving@brf.org.uk** or call us on **01235 462305**.

*Not all mobile phone networks support text giving. If yours doesn't, your message won't be delivered, and you won't be charged. You can always donate online at brf.org.uk/donate. Our privacy policy is available at brf.org.uk/privacy.

YOU CAN DONATE TO MESSY CHURCH AT ANY TIME BY TEXT

Text 'MESSY' followed by your donation amount to 70450 (e.g. text 'MESSY 3' to 70450 to donate £3). Texts cost your chosen donation amount plus one standard rate message.*

@MessyChurchBRF @messychurch

Aike writes...

Welcome to Get Messy! Volume 2

Get Messy! Volume 2 contains twelve session outlines for Messy Churches. This volume takes you through the basic themes of Christianity, including: Who is God? Who is Jesus? Who is the Holy Spirit? The material includes the key Christian festivals: Christmas – God entering the world as Jesus; Easter – exploring Jesus' last supper and why Christians celebrate Communion; and Pentecost – the arrival and gift of the Holy Spirit. The sessions also cover God's best ways of living, demonstrated through the life and stories of Jesus, with themes on love, grace, mercy and forgiveness. It also includes God's plan to save everyone, a challenge to follow Jesus and trust God with a new direction, exploring following and belonging to Jesus through baptism. The themes in this volume are especially suited to Messy Churches that have just started or that may have people who are at the start of their journey of discovering Jesus. For Messy Churches that have been gathering for longer, the sessions provide the perfect opportunity for your Messy Church to explore the sacraments of Communion and invite people to a commitment to follow Jesus through baptism.

How to use Get Messy!

Other than those on the key Christian festivals – Christmas, Easter and Pentecost – the sessions stand alone, so they can be done in any order. Feel free to choose topics that are most suitable for your context.

It's important to remember that any resource is just a springboard, and we hope that you will creatively adapt ideas for your Messy Church. If the themes in this edition are not the right fit for you, as we're all at different stages on the Messy Church journey, we have a massive back catalogue of resources available at **messychurch.org.uk**.

A huge thank you to our writers, who have taken the time to create and test-drive these sessions, especially those who are writing for the first time. Each one includes a Bible story and some pointers to get your team thinking about how to talk about the theme during the activities. We've added some 'I wonder?' open-ended questions for each activity and during the celebration, to help people of all ages to engage with the topics.

We suggest you take time at the start of your planning meetings to pray, reflect on where you noticed God at work in your previous session and if anyone had any 'God conversations' that might need following up. Then read the Bible together and be curious about which words or verses stand out. This will help your team talk about the key Bible themes that you wish to share during the activity time and will provide you with a fantastic opportunity for discipleship within your team. You'll find a choice of ten activities, designed for a range of ages and abilities, with both indoor and Messy Church Goes Wild (outdoor) activity suggestions. Remember you don't have to do them all! We're also thinking about how we can be more eco-friendly with our activities, so try to reduce your waste, reuse what you already have in the back of your church cupboard before buying anything new and think about how any craft items can be recycled after Messy Church.

Additional templates and table activity signs can be found at **messychurch.org.uk/getmessyvol2-2878**.

The social action idea can help your Messy Church be church throughout the month, encouraging people to put into action the Bible theme. In the celebration section you'll find ideas to retell the Bible story in an engaging way, together with a prayer, plus song suggestions. Finally, to help you with hospitality, we've included mealtime card question ideas (you can download this in the support material), designed to keep the conversation flowing when you gather to eat, together with a meal suggestion.

Remember to check out the stories and articles that accompany these sessions on our social media, blogs, e-newsletters and website.

 Messy Church-BRF
 @messychurch
 @MessyChurchBRF
 @MessyChurchBRF
 @MessyChurchBRF

Visit messychurch.org.uk/getmessyvol2-2878 to download all sorts of extra content for these sessions, including photos, templates, table signs, mealtime cards and a session planning template!

Additional copies can be purchased at **brfonline.org.uk/new-get-messy** or using the order form on page 72.

Session material: September
Who is God? What is God like?
by Sharon Sampson

Bible story for prep

Psalm 139:1–18 (NIV)

You have searched me, Lord, and you know me. You know when I sit and when I rise; you perceive my thoughts from afar. You discern my going out and my lying down; you are familiar with all my ways. Before a word is on my tongue you, Lord, know it completely. You hem me in behind and before, and you lay your hand upon me. Such knowledge is too wonderful for me, too lofty for me to attain.

Where can I go from your Spirit? Where can I flee from your presence? If I go up to the heavens, you are there; if I make my bed in the depths, you are there. If I rise on the wings of the dawn, if I settle on the far side of the sea, even there your hand will guide me, your right hand will hold me fast. If I say, 'Surely the darkness will hide me and the light become night around me,' even the darkness will not be dark to you; the night will shine like the day, for darkness is as light to you.

For you created my inmost being; you knit me together in my mother's womb. I praise you because I am fearfully and wonderfully made; your works are wonderful, I know that full well. My frame was not hidden from you when I was made in the secret place, when I was woven together in the depths of the earth. Your eyes saw my unformed body; all the days ordained for me were written in your book before one of them came to be. How precious to me are your thoughts, God! How vast is the sum of them! Were I to count them, they would outnumber the grains of sand – when I awake, I am still with you.

Pointers

Some people might think, 'How can we know a God we can't see or touch?' But the Bible is full of descriptions of his character. One such place is in Psalm 139, which includes these phrases:

- 'You know me' – God is not some distant figure but someone who knows everything about us, the good and the bad, and still loves us.
- 'You are there' – God is always with us, waiting and wanting to be part of our lives.
- 'Your right hand will guide me' – if we choose to believe, God's Spirit will help us through life.
- 'Your hand will hold me fast' – no matter what trials we go through, God holds us and support us.
- 'The night will shine like the day' – God can shine light into the darkest of times in our lives.
- 'You created my inmost being' – God is the one almighty creator, who created us, for a purpose. Each one of us is precious to God.

How does this session help people grow in Christ?

Some people envisage God as a remote being whose only interaction with people is to rain down fire when they misbehave. This session is designed to help us get to know the real God. God is not an old man with a long beard, sitting on a cloud, dishing out punishment. Instead, God is the creator both of the universe and of the very breath inside us. God knows us intimately. Hopefully we will discover that we can have a personal relationship with God.

Add value

Mealtime card

- Before today, what did you think God was like?
- Do you like to chat to God?
- When do you feel closest to God?

Question to start and end the session

So… if you could ask God one question, what would it be?

Social action idea

God created an amazing world. How can we care for it better? Challenge your Messy Church to do a litter pick.

Activities

1. God is our creator – clay and construction craft

You will need: a globe (optional); blue and green material; clay; aprons; paper plates; simple tools; washing-up facilities; construction bricks

Make a giant earth on the floor from the material provided, or from what you can find outside. Ask people to 'create' something out of clay and place it on the earth. It could be themselves, or an animal, or they can be like God and create something completely new. You could also have construction bricks for people to make buildings.

Talk about how God created all of the amazing world around us, and God created us too. We are all unique and special, God has made us for a purpose. God is the ultimate creator and loves it when we are creative too.

I wonder... what's your favourite part of the natural world?

2. God is light in the darkness – Messy craft

You will need: black card; scissors; white, yellow and orange paints; cling film; stubby brushes or toothbrushes

Paint 'God is light in the darkness' on one corner of the paper. Use the brushes, dipped in white paint, to spray white stars on to the black card. Blob on a circle of orange and yellow paint for the sun. Spread cling film on top, use your hands to squish all the paint around into a swirling circle. Finally, remove the cling film.

Talk about how God's first recorded words were 'Let there be light' (Genesis 1:3). Just as placing a candle in a dark room can remove all fear and uncertainty, God can be a light in our lives, bringing us comfort and helping us through the dark times we all go through from time to time. All we have to do is talk to God and let God fill us with hope and peace.

I wonder... what situations need God's light at the moment?

Additional copies can be purchased at **brfonline.org.uk/new-get-messy** or using the order form on page 72.

3. God is all-powerful – crocodile craft

You will need: wooden pegs; green paint; googly eyes; green paper; green pipe cleaners; scissors; glue

Before the session, paint the pegs green so they can dry in time. Fold up a strip of green paper and stick it on the peg, and attach the googly eyes. Cut and bend the legs and stick on or simply poke them through.

Talk about how a Nile crocodile has the most powerful bite of the animal kingdom, at 5,000 psi, and yet it has tiny bumps along its jaw line which are more sensitive than human fingertips. It can snap at its prey but also carry its babies in its mouth. In the same way, God is all powerful but is also gentle. Matthew 19:26 says: 'With man this is impossible, but with God all things are possible.'

I wonder… what impossible situation would you like to see God change?

4. God is love – nativity collage

You will need: A4 card; hay; strips of cardboard or sticks; coloured paper; bits of material; sticky stars; glue; pens

Make a collage of the nativity scene.

Talk about how God loves us so much that he sent his only Son down to earth, so that through Jesus we could get to know him better. God could have come as a conquering king in a palace, but instead he came as a vulnerable baby. We might think it is hard to know what God is like, but all we have to do is look at who Jesus is and what he is like.

I wonder… what characteristics of Jesus do you like best?

5. God is our Father – house rules craft

You will need: coloured card; white card; coloured pens; glue; scissors

Make a poster to put up at home to remind you of your house rules. Rules to keep you safe, to be kind and considerate to others, to keep you close to your Father God. Leave room to glue on coloured card as a frame.

Talk about Jesus calling God 'Abba', which is like 'Daddy'. Jesus taught us to pray to God by starting with 'Our Father', so we can think of God not only as Jesus' dad but ours too. A good father protects, plays with and takes care of his children, and he also guides them and gives them boundaries and rules to help them become kind and thoughtful adults.

I wonder… where can you place your house rules so guests can see them? Try to use them to start a God-conversation.

6. God is eternal – drawing

You will need: printed copies of the template; pens

Print copies of the template. People can colour it in, add figures, animals, windows, clouds, other buildings and the words 'God is eternal'.

Talk about how God created time and space, and is outside of time itself. God is beyond all that we can imagine and cannot be measured. God has always been and will always be. God is a mystery and eternal, infinite, like the steps in the template. And the best bit is that God has promised that we can be with God for eternity, if we choose to believe.

I wonder... what questions do you have about this?

7. God is good – food game

You will need: blindfold; plates; good food (chocolate buttons, grapes, jam, dried apricots); bad food (slice of lemon, dry cereal, pickle, coffee powder); spoons

Check for food allergies before beginning and adjust accordingly. Blindfold someone and then using a spoon, give them one of the foods to try. Can they guess what the food is? Ask them if they think it is a bad food or a good food.

Talk about Psalm 34:8, where it says: 'Taste and see that the Lord is good; blessed is the one who takes refuge in him.' God is good. Stick with God and you will be blessed. Stay away from bad things, for they only bring trouble and heartache.

I wonder... is anything causing you heartache at the moment?

8. God is Spirit – race

You will need: large paper fish; trays for wafting; start and finish lines marked out

Lay the large paper fish down at the start line and give each racer a tray (or a thick piece of A4 card). The racers must make their fish move from the start to the finish line only by wafting air over it (using the tray); they cannot touch the fish.

Talk about how God the Father is not a human being with a physical body like ours. God is spirit, which is more like the wind. This allows God to be everywhere all at the same time. The Bible tells us that God has breathed life into all living things, which includes fish and us.

I wonder... what questions do you have about God?

9. God is truth – quiz

You will need: true/false quiz questions; line on the floor; sign saying TRUE; sign saying FALSE; something to give us a small prize to everyone

One person reads out the questions. To answer, people jump to either the TRUE or the FALSE sides of the room, depending on what they think the answer is. If you have a large group and want to make it competitive, people can sit out when they get an answer wrong. At the end, give everyone a small prize.

Talk about how God is 'omniscient', which means all-knowing, in the sense that God is aware of the past, present and future. Nothing takes God by surprise. God's knowledge is total. God knows all that there is to know about you – your good and bad bits – and he loves you anyway. Exodus 34:6 says: 'The Lord, the compassionate and gracious God, slow to anger, abounding in love and faithfulness.' God is gracious, which means that God loves us even if we don't deserve it. That is why everyone got a prize today, not just the winners.

I wonder... do you think it's fair that everyone got a prize today?

10. God is our guide – obstacle course

You will need: blindfold; obstacles; feather; water spray; chocolate buttons

Set up an obstacle course, but instead of 'Start' and 'Finish', use 'Alpha' and 'Omega'. Blindfold someone and ask them if they would like a guide. Have people dotted around the course, ready to spray with water, tickle with a feather, or offer a chocolate button. The guide, if chosen, can steer them away from the obstacles, water and feathers and towards the chocolate. Obstacle ideas: under a table, through a hoop, under a blanket, over a bench, balance a cup of water on head, under a pool noodle, step through tyres, crawl through a tunnel of chairs.

Talk about how God wants to be our guide through life, but we can choose if we want to listen to God. God is always there for us. He said, 'I am the Alpha and the Omega... who is, and who was, and who is to come, the Almighty' (Revelation 1:8).

I wonder... what do you want to say to God?

Celebration

Prepare a large box with a hole in it, big enough that someone can get their arm in to pull out objects. Write 'Who is God?' on the outside. Wrap each object in a Bible verse. Also draw a large hand-palm print on a wall, ready for an interactive prayer later. Place coloured pens nearby.

Start wearing a long white beard and say, 'How many of you, before today, thought that God was an old man with a long white beard, sitting on a cloud?' Take it off and say, 'Hopefully, you now know God a lot better. In this box, I have some clues to what God is like. Will you help me work out the clues?' Invite people to take out an object, others to guess what it says about God and then they read the Bible verse to confirm it. Encourage everyone to expand on the scripture. If they don't, you can do so using the ideas below. If you have a big board or wall, you might like to stick up big words, such as truth, love, light.

Objects and verses to use

Torch: 1 John 1:5 – 'God is light; in him there is no darkness at all.' Sometimes we will be sad, lonely or miserable. It can feel like a very dark place to be. But we don't need to sit in the dark by ourselves. God is always there beside us. We can talk to him, and if we listen carefully, he can help us find a way out of the dark into the light.

Crocodile: 1 Chronicles 29:11 – 'Yours, Lord, is the greatness and the power and the glory and the majesty and the splendour.' A Nile crocodile has the most powerful bite of the animal kingdom and yet its jaw is more sensitive than human fingertips. In the same way God is all powerful but can be gentle and sensitive with us too.

Ruler: Matthew 6:8 – 'Your Father knows what you need before you ask him.' God is not just Jesus' Father but ours too. And like any good father, God gives us rules and boundaries to keep us happy and safe.

Paper pinwheel: Job 33:4 – 'The Spirit of God has made me; the breath of the Almighty gives me life.' God the Father is not a human being with a physical body like ours. He is spirit, which is more like the wind. This allows God to be everywhere all at the same time.

Chocolate: Psalm 34:8 – 'Taste and see that the Lord is good; blessed is the one who takes refuge in him.' God is good. Stick with God and you will be blessed. Stay away from bad things for they only bring trouble.

Heart-shaped object: John 3:16 – 'For God so loved the world that he gave his one and only Son, that whoever believes in him shall not perish but have eternal life.' There is no greater love than giving up your life or that of your child. That is how much God loves us.

Eternity symbol: Psalm 90:2 – 'Before the mountains were born or you brought forth the whole world, from everlasting to everlasting you are God.' It is hard to imagine, but God is outside time and space. God has always existed and will always exist in the future. The great news is that we can be with God for eternity too.

Blindfold: Psalm 27:11 – 'Teach me your way, Lord; lead me in a straight path.' God wants to be our guide through life, but we can choose if we listen or not. We can go through life with a blindfold on or with God at our side.

Bible with hand-palm cut-out: Exodus 34:6 – 'The Lord, the compassionate and gracious God, slow to anger, abounding in love and faithfulness.' God is all all-knowing; nothing takes God by surprise. God's knowledge is total. God knows all that there is to know about us, our good and bad bits, and loves us anyway.

Construction bricks: Isaiah 64:8 – 'Yet you, Lord, are our Father. We are the clay, you are the potter; we are all the work of your hand.' God created us. We are all unique and very special to God, who has made us for a purpose.

Prayer

Father God, we know that if you have a fridge, our pictures are on it. If you have a wallet, our photos are in it. Thank you for sending us flowers every spring and a sunrise every morning. Thank you for being there whenever we want to talk. You could live anywhere in the universe, but you chose our hearts, and the Bible tells us that you have written our names on the palms of your hands. Amen.

I invite you to come and write your name on the giant hand-palm. As you wait your turn, I will play quiet music and you might like to think of all the things we have learnt about God today. In your mind, chat to God and ask for a picture or word of something from today that God wants to highlight to you or wants you to take away from our time together.

I wonder...

- What surprised you most about God's character?
- In what ways are you most like God?

Song suggestions

'Our God is a great big God' – Nigel and Jo Hemming
'My God is so big, so strong and so mighty' – Ruth Harms Calkin
'He's got the whole world in his hands' – Mission Praise #225
'Made for this' – Maker Fun Factory
'Written on the palm of God's hand' – Fischy Music

Meal suggestions

Buffet with labels on each plate: light, power, creator, love, good, Spirit, guide, truth, Father, eternal. You could use round bread or wraps, and place food on top to make faces. What do you think God looks like?

Download support material at **messychurch.org.uk/getmessyvol2-2878**

Session material: October
Who is Jesus?
It's all about love
by Lydia Harrison

Bible story for prep

John 13:34 (NIV)

'A new command I give you: love one another. As I have loved you, so you must love one another.'

Pointers

We love because God first loved us. Love comes in many forms, and there are many different ways to show love. It is important to remember that we are called to love people who are different from us, who lead different lives and who have different opinions.

There are all sorts of different viewpoints around Halloween – some people engage with it, some people see it as a 'celebration of evil' and some people take it and put a positive spin on it, reminding us that the light of Christ shines even in the darkest of times. However we feel about Halloween, we remember that the power of God's love and light overcomes the evil and darkness in the world. We can join in with spreading God's light, hope and love.

- God calls us to love one another – not just people who are like us, but ALL people.
- The light and love of God shines in the darkness. How do we show that light and love to everyone?
- We are called to love our enemies. What would the world look like if we took this more seriously?

How does this session help people grow in Christ?

Jesus reminds us that the commandment to love one another as he has loved us is the most important. We are also reminded that this love extends to people outside our normal friendship and church groups; it is for absolutely everyone, yes, even those with whom we disagree or do not like! How we can extend this love to our enemies today? How different would the world be if we got on with the business of loving one another, challenging hate and reaching out with peace?

Add value

Mealtime card
- Who might you class as your 'enemies'?
- In what ways might you show love to your 'enemies' this week?
- In what ways can you shine with God's love this week?

Question to start and end the session
So… what does it mean to love one another, even our enemies? What would the world look like if we did this?

Social action idea
Write to your local MP to remind them that when they are making decisions, they need to consider the needs of all people and make decisions with love, grace and peace. Collect items for your local food bank, and donate these as a way of reaching out in love to those in need.

Additional copies can be purchased at **brfonline.org.uk/new-get-messy** or using the order form on page 72.

Activities

1. Mending hurts

You will need: a large heart-shaped piece of card; plasters; pens. Or if you wanted to make individual hearts for people to take home, some smaller hearts and smaller plasters

Encourage adults and children to stick some plasters to the card. You could write on the heart people or situations that need God's love and light, such as relationships that need healing or prayers for our enemies. Pray together that God's love and light will shine in all these things.

Talk about how Jesus' first commandment is that we need to love one another, just as he has loved us. Some situations in our lives may need healing in order that love can be rebuilt. Prayer is a great first step in this.

I wonder... what situation would you like to pray about?

2. Dancing leaves collage

You will need: leaves from outside – collect a few days before so they can dry; acrylic or poster paint; paint brushes; eye stickers or googly eyes; pens; large backing paper

Choose a leaf and paint it with acrylic or poster paint. Place this paint side down on the poster paper and make a print. Add arms, legs and eyes to it, and write underneath it a word or phrase which summarises what love is for you.

Talk about how there are different ways to show love.

I wonder... how might you show love this week?

3. Lanterns

You will need: paper/thin card; stickers; glue; sticky tape; scissors; electric tealights

Fold the paper in half lengthways, and from the folded edge, cut strips along the whole length of the paper, leaving 2–3 cm before the edge. You should have room for around 8–10 cuts on an A4 piece. Unfold this and make it into a cylinder by bringing the two short ends of the paper together – stick it together. Decorate with stickers or drawings (if drawing, do this before you stick it together). Make another strip for the handle, and two strips that cross over at the bottom of the lantern which will hold the tealight.

Talk about how the world would become a brighter place if we all loved one another like Jesus asks us to.

I wonder... what dark situations or places need Christ's light to shine?

Download support material at **messychurch.org.uk/getmessyvol2-2878**

4. Campfire biscuits

You will need: digestives or other circular biscuits; mini chocolate fingers or shortbread fingers to represent logs (Matchmaker chocolates work well); mini marshmallows; runny icing to glue it all together; strawberry laces to represent fire

Using the digestive or circular biscuit as a base, put a layer of icing on it, then make a triangle with the long thin biscuits. Then place marshmallows around this, and drape the laces across the top to make it look like flames.

Talk about how even the smallest flame can make a massive difference and brighten up a room. When we love everyone, this love spreads around and makes the world a brighter place.

I wonder... when was the last time you watched a campfire burning? How did it make you feel?

5. Scratch art cities

You will need: A4 or A5 scratch art paper; scratch sticks; pens

You may need to first draw a template on the scratch art paper for people to copy. Use the scratch art paper to make a picture of your village, community or town. As you scratch the black away, you will start to see colour shining through.

Talk about how you could use this as a mindful, prayerful activity where you pray for everyone who lives there, even the people you do not get on with.

I wonder... how could you use this picture as a prayer activity?

6. Prayer walk

You will need: a safe place to go for a walk outside

Organise a walk through your community, stopping at key places to pray for the people who live, work and play there. Consider health and safety, e.g. crossing the road.

Talk about how even a small action can have a massive impact, but we might not always see this straight away. Prayer is powerful, and we should keep praying.

I wonder... who is God prompting us to pray for?

7. Gratitude pumpkin

You will need: orange strips of paper with holes in each end; split pins; green leaves; green pipe cleaners; pens

Write on each strip of paper something you are thankful for, such as your favourite food, your loved ones or something good happening in your life. Put the split pin through the holes in one side of the strips, then bring them together into an arch. Put the other split pin in the other end and fasten them together. Glue the leaf on top. Alternatively, you could carve some real pumpkins with smiley faces and write on them things you are thankful for.

Talk about how even when you're having a really bad day, there are still things to be thankful for.

I wonder… what made you smile today? Give thanks for that.

8. Hidden message

You will need: white crayons; white paper; watercolour paints

Using the white crayon, write a message on the paper that says something about God's love. This could simply be the word 'love' or something more detailed. Use the watercolour paint to make a pattern on the paper, and watch as the wax resists the paint, leaving the message clear.

Talk about how good it is to spread words of love, and how these can make a difference to those around us.

I wonder… how does it feel to spread words of love? How can kind words make a difference?

9. Left out?

You will need: as many heart-shaped pieces of paper as there are participants; music that stops and starts

Place the heart-shaped pieces of paper on the floor and get people to dance around them to the music. When the music stops, each person has to stand on a heart. The rule is only one person can stand on each heart! As each round begins, take a heart away until only one is left. If a person is not stood on a heart, they are out. The last person stood on the heart, wins!

Talk about how it felt to be left out? I wonder how it feels to be left out of something because someone disagrees with you, or even counts you as an enemy? Remember this feeling as you go about your daily lives, as a reminder to include people who are left out.

I wonder… how does it feel to be left out?

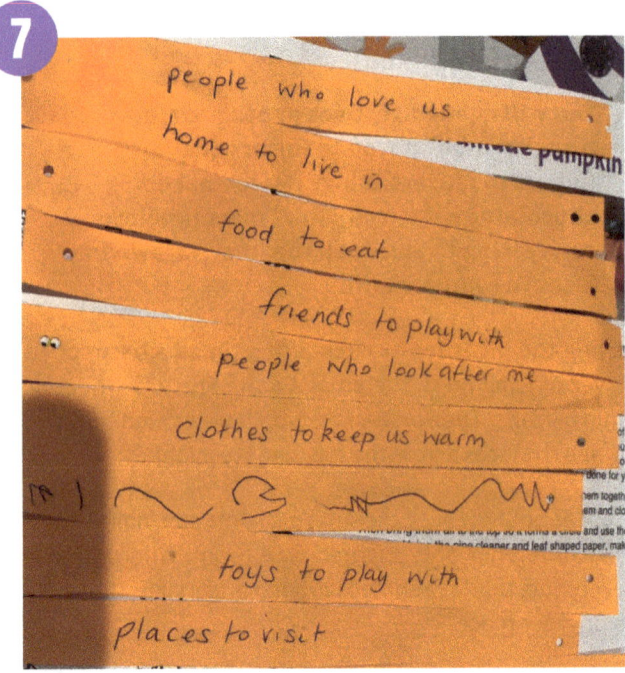

10. Building love

You will need: mini marshmallows; dried spaghetti pasta

Use the marshmallows and the spaghetti to construct something that represents love and inclusion, such as a heart or a building where everyone is welcome.

Talk about how including even people we don't like is important in God's kingdom.

I wonder… who is God asking me to include or invite to Messy Church?

Celebration

You will need your prayer lanterns (activity 3) and hearts (activity 1) and a banner saying, 'Welcome'.

Jesus commanded us to love one another with the same love that he loves us.

The gospel message is that God loves us so much that he sent his only Son that we might have life in all its fullness. This love is massive and life-changing! It brings people together, it heals, it restores, and it is for everyone! Even the people we are vastly different from! Even, and especially, those we do not get on with!

Jesus warns us that greeting only the people who we class as our own is dangerous, and he reminds us that we need to welcome everybody.

Using the welcome banner as the front runner, start a conga line that goes round the room or the building, even going outside if it is safe. As you go round, chant 'Love one another' or 'God's love is for everyone!' Hold your lanterns as you do so, as a sign and reminder that when we love one another, the world is a brighter and kinder place.

Remind people that there are different opinions about most things in the world, but Halloween is a great reminder of the power and love of God, a reminder that his love casts our fear and the light that shines from God overcomes all darkness. However you celebrate (or not!) Halloween, remember that God is always with us and that the saints who have lived before us have shone with God's love, so let's be a shining example to those around us.

I wonder…

- Who is missing from our group today? How can we invite them next time?
- What might we need to do differently if people who are different from us come and join in?
- How might the world look if everyone was loved and included?

Prayer
Lift up the heart-shaped card with plasters on together, and pray the following:

Lord of love, we thank you for your healing and inclusive love.
We pray for all the situations we have placed on these hearts, knowing that you hear all our prayers.
May we each know love. *(Point to ourselves)*
May we walk in the way of love. *(Walk on the spot)*
May we reach out to everyone with love. *(Reach out arms)*
May we light up our world with love. *(Do a circle shape with our arms)*
Each and every day.
Amen.

Song suggestions
'A new commandment' – Roy Crabtree
'Jesus loves me' – Chris Tomlin
'Love, love, love' – Fischy Music
'Welcome everybody' – Fischy Music

Meal suggestions
Stone soup is the name given to a wide variety of hearty meat-and-vegetable soups that stems from a European folktale about community sharing. Stone soup typically features humble but delicious ingredients, like potatoes, peas, cabbage and affordable cuts of beef or chicken. Maybe invite your community to bring a couple of vegetables each so we can make a stone soup together. Accompany this with bread. For afters, possibly have fruit salad that follows the same sort of ideas as the stone soup.

Additional copies can be purchased at **brfonline.org.uk/new-get-messy** or using the order form on page 72.

Session material: November
Who is Jesus?
It's all about grace
by Anne Offler and Sharon Pritchard

Bible story for prep

Matthew 20:1–16 (NIV)

'For the kingdom of heaven is like a landowner who went out early in the morning to hire workers for his vineyard. He agreed to pay them a denarius for the day and sent them into his vineyard.

'About nine in the morning he went out and saw others standing in the market-place doing nothing. He told them, "You also go and work in my vineyard, and I will pay you whatever is right." So they went.

'He went out again about noon and about three in the afternoon and did the same thing. About five in the afternoon he went out and found still others standing around. He asked them, "Why have you been standing here all day long doing nothing?"

'"Because no one has hired us," they answered.

'He said to them, "You also go and work in my vineyard."

'When evening came, the owner of the vineyard said to his foreman, "Call the workers and pay them their wages, beginning with the last ones hired and going on to the first."

'The workers who were hired about five in the afternoon came and each received a denarius. So when those came who were hired first, they expected to receive more. But each one of them also received a denarius. When they received it, they began to grumble against the landowner. "These who were hired last worked only one hour," they said, "and you have made them equal to us who have borne the burden of the work and the heat of the day."

'But he answered one of them, "I am not being unfair to you, friend. Didn't you agree to work for a denarius? Take your pay and go. I want to give the one who was hired last the same as I gave you. Don't I have the right to do what I want with my own money? Or are you envious because I am generous?"

'So the last will be first, and the first will be last.'

Pointers

- The story is about workers in the vineyard who were happy to be employed for the wages offered.
- They felt a sense of injustice when those working for part of the day received the same wages.
- Does the sense of injustice cloud their feelings of gratitude, and possibly generosity, that both themselves and others were being paid so that they too could eat and pay bills?
- Jesus is telling this story for more than just illustrating a sense of justice.
- Did all the workers deserve what they were paid?
- This story illustrates that we don't deserve Jesus' love but his grace sees beyond our poor choices and enables our relationship with him to grow.

How does this session help people grow in Christ?

This story is a picture of how God values and is gracious to everyone, offering us more than we deserve, because God loves us. God sent Jesus to show us God's best way to live and to restore us to a right relationship with God. God's grace is a free gift, but we have to choose to accept it and follow Jesus. This session challenges people to consider what God's grace looks like.

Add value

Mealtime card
- Did all the workers in this story feel they have been fairly/unfairly treated?
- Why do you think Jesus told this story?
- How does this story show Jesus' grace?

Question to start and end the session
So… where do we see the grace of Jesus at work?

Social action idea
Think about situations in your area or globally that seem to be unfair and consider supporting a charity or agency trying to help or write to your MP highlighting the issue.

Activities

1. Let's get to work!

You will need: a print-out of the sheet of the different jobs with letters next to them – cut these up and place the cards around your space; copies of the grid to be filled in by each person

Give each person a grid and ask them to match up the people doing the jobs with the cards around the room, writing the letter on the card into the grid. The phrase 'Is it fair?' should be spelled out when all the letters have been collected.

Talk about people going to work and the different jobs that people do.

I wonder… why do people go to work? In today's story some of the workers thought their pay was not fair. What do you think?

2. Gracious grapes

You will need: purple card or cardboard tubes coloured in purple; scissors; leaves (paper, real, artificial); a branch (real or cardboard twisted to look like a branch); felt-tip pens; sticky tape or glue dots

Colour the card purple if needed – you could also colour it light green for the grapes. Cut the tube or card into strips and make a circle, securing it with sticky tape or glue dots. Repeat until you have a few circles to be grapes.

Arrange the grapes together to make a bunch and secure. Attach some leaves to the top and then attach the bunch of grapes to the branch to look like grapes hanging from a vine.

Talk about how the workers in the field were picking grapes – have you ever picked grapes? They grow on a vine in a vineyard. They need lots of water to grow and lots of sunshine.

I wonder… why do you think some grapes are purple and some are green? Which are your favourite?

3. Salt dough money

You will need: plain flour; salt; water; a bowl; a measuring spoon or cup; rolling pin; cutters (optional); a plate

Into the bowl put flour, salt and water in the ratio 2:2:1. Mix it up to make a dough. Roll out the dough and make coin shapes. Mark the 'coins' with your design. Put them on the plate to dry or to take home to bake slowly later.

Talk about what we use money to buy.

I wonder… why did landowner in Jesus' parable pay all of the workers the same amount of money? Did they deserve the same wages?

4. Treading grapes

You will need: a large container or small paddling pool containing a number of small sponges full of water; towels; a timer

Introduce the old-fashioned grape treading machine when people squeezed the juice from the grapes by standing on them. Invite some 'workers' to tread on the grapes (sponges) with their bare feet to squeeze the juice (water) out. Do this for two minutes without stopping.

Talk about how tiring it was to get the juice from the grapes. The workers in Jesus' story had to work hard.

I wonder… do you think the workers were happy to have a job that day?

5. Fruit salad smoothie

You will need: soft fruits, such as strawberries, bananas, blackberries, mango, pineapple (make sure you wash/peel them!); plastic or butter knives; chopping boards; liquidisers or a food mill; milk (or alternative); honey; plastic drinking cups; straws

Chop the fruit into small pieces and place them in the liquidizer or food mill. Add some milk and blend it all into a smoothie. Carefully pour smoothie into the drinking cups, add straws and enjoy.

Talk about when the fruits are mixed together into a smoothie it gives a delicious flavour.

I wonder… what the wine the workers were making in the vineyard tasted like? What do you like to drink on special occasions? What's your favourite smoothie combination?

6. Invisible ink grace

You will need: sheets of white paper with the word 'GRACE' painted on them with bicarbonate of soda, all dried; grape juice or blackcurrant squash (undiluted); paint brushes; cotton buds

Mix together equal amounts of bicarbonate of soda and water, this mixture will be your invisible ink. Paint the word GRACE onto the paper using the mixture and a cotton bud. Leave to dry completely. Paint over the white paper using the grape juice. The word should be revealed, can you tell what it is? It is the word 'GRACE'.

Talk about how grace is something invisible, but is always there. Jesus shows us his grace when we ask him. Grace reveals itself when we need it most.

I wonder… can you think of a situation when someone has shown you grace? How did that feel?

7. Woven together

You will need: different coloured wool or thread (each colour representing a characteristic of Jesus, e.g. red – love, blue – forgiveness, green – kindness, yellow – grace, purple – mercy, pink – compassion); blunt tapestry type needles; plastic canvas or aida cut into squares or rectangles; scissors

Weave different coloured threads in and out of the holes crossing over one another.

Talk about how each of the coloured threads make up the picture or pattern just like the different characteristics of Jesus make up who he is.

I wonder… what coloured threads would we weave together to show our characteristics?

Download support material at **messychurch.org.uk/getmessyvol2-2878**

8. Lego challenge

You will need: two identical small sets of Lego (one with the instructions removed); ideally two tables so that groups cannot see others working

Split into two groups and then give each group a set of Lego, without discussing the contents of the pack. Invite the groups to make up the model and see who can finish it first.

Talk about how much easier the model was to build for the group that had the instructions.

I wonder… was this game a fair contest? Why? Why not? Is everything in life fair? Can you think of a situation at the moment where you want to say, 'That's not fair'?

9. Matching pairs card game

You will need: a copy of the matching pairs game PDF printed out on card and each card cut out

Place all the cards face down on the table. Ask the children to choose one card and turn it over, choose another and if they match as a pair put them together and set aside. If the cards do not match, they must both be turned face down again for the next person's turn.

Talk about which cards you can find. Can you find the angry workers card? What do you think would make them happy again? Can you find the grace card? Grace is Jesus' goodness to us – even when we don't get things right, he forgives us.

I wonder… what would make the angry workers happy? How did the workers who only started work at the end of the day, but got paid in full, feel?

10. Emoji prayers

You will need: a copy of the emoji prayers PDF for each person; pens

Instructions are on the PDF. Choose one or more of the emojis and write the name of the person you would like to pray for, or you own name on one of the emojis, i.e. 'Dear God, we pray for my gran, who is sick at the moment. Amen.'

Talk about how emojis show how someone is feeling.

I wonder… what emojis do you think the workers in the Bible story might have used?

Photocopying not permitted except under the CLA Church Licence.

Celebration

What a story we had today – a story Jesus told a long time ago. In the story there were lots of people hoping they would be picked to help make the wine. They got out of bed early *(mime yawning and stretching)* and went to the marketplace to wait to see if they would be chosen *(people looks hopeful)*. Very soon the boss came along and chose some of the people to help him *(indicate to one third of the group and tell them they have been chosen)*. These people were very happy *(celebrate waving arms in the air and smiling)*. They would get paid that day and be able to buy food and pay the bills. The others leftover – well they had to settle down and wait to see if anyone else would come along to give them work *(these people look sad)*.

At about lunchtime the boss came back again and looked at the people who were still waiting for work *(people look hopeful)*. He told some of them *(indicate another third of the group)* they could go and work in the vineyard and off they went *(wave arms in the air and smile)*. The people left were sad. They might not get a job that day and no job meant no pay. No money meant no food. Oh dear!

The people left with no job were just about to go home when the boss came back again and told them they could go and work in the vineyard. They were so happy!

At the end of the day all of the workers gathered together and the boss came to pay them. He gave them all the same amount of money *(optional – give out chocolate coins or small wrapped sweets or cardboard tokens)*.

The workers who went to pick the grapes last were very happy. The workers who did half of the day were quite happy, but the workers who had worked all day grumbled.

I wonder...

- Did the workers who started first thing think the others had been given more than they deserved?
- Should some workers have been given half of the day's pay or some just a little bit?
- What was Jesus trying to say through this story? Maybe he was trying to show that the workers didn't get what they deserved; they were given more. Perhaps he wants us to think about how he doesn't give us what we deserve, especially when we get things wrong, but because he loves us he is generous and kind and forgives us. We sometimes get so much more than we deserve from him. I wonder if this is Jesus' grace?

Prayer

Prepare five cube boxes to be either held or stacked as the prayer is said. On one face of each box write the letters J E S U S. Turn the boxes to the next face and write C A R E S. Turn the boxes again and draw emojis of happy, sad, angry, confused and surprised one on each face. Lastly turn again and write G R A C E.

Ask for five people to come and help with the prayers. Give them a box each, and ask them to hold them in order to spell the first word – JESUS. Ask them to turn each box at the end of each of the part of the prayer. (This can also be done with very large cuboid boxes which can be stood one on top of the other and turned for each part of the prayer.) As we pray, the words on the boxes will change as they are turned.

Start with the boxes showing the word J E S U S.

Lord Jesus, thank you for our time together today and the things we have thought about. *Turn boxes to show the word C A R E S.*

Thank you that you care about each one of us and challenge us to think about the things we do. *Turn boxes to show the emojis.*

Sometimes we are happy, sometimes we are sad.

Sometimes we are angry or confused especially when things seem to be unfair.

Sometimes we are surprised, especially when you still love us even when we don't deserve it.

Turn boxes to show the word G R A C E.

Thank you for your grace shown to us because you love us.

Song suggestions

'This is amazing grace' – Bethel Music Kids
'King of me' – Rend Co. Kids
'What a mighty God we serve' – Kids Praise and Worship

Meal suggestions

Roasted vegetable tray bake. For this you can use any vegetables you have, such as peppers, butternut squash or pumpkin, potatoes, onions, carrots, parsnips. As this session includes a story with a vineyard, you might like to include purple and white/green foods to represent the grapes. You could use aubergines, purple carrots and purple and white potatoes, beetroot, purple and white onions, purple cabbage, etc. You could have purple and white/green cupcakes ready for dessert.

You could serve the fruit salad smoothie as part of your meal.

Session material: December
God enters the world
by Sharon Sampson

 PDF DOWNLOAD    MESSY CHURCH AT HOME    MESSY CHURCH GOES WILD

Bible story for prep

Matthew 1:18–25 (NIV)

This is how the birth of Jesus the Messiah came about: his mother Mary was pledged to be married to Joseph, but before they came together, she was found to be pregnant through the Holy Spirit. Because Joseph her husband was faithful to the law, and yet did not want to expose her to public disgrace, he had in mind to divorce her quietly.

But after he had considered this, an angel of the Lord appeared to him in a dream and said, 'Joseph son of David, do not be afraid to take Mary home as your wife, because what is conceived in her is from the Holy Spirit. She will give birth to a son, and you are to give him the name Jesus, because he will save his people from their sins.'

All this took place to fulfil what the Lord had said through the prophet: 'The virgin will conceive and give birth to a son, and they will call him Immanuel' (which means 'God with us').

When Joseph woke up, he did what the angel of the Lord had commanded him and took Mary home as his wife. But he did not consummate their marriage until she gave birth to a son. And he gave him the name Jesus.

Pointers

An angel brings a message. A little baby is born in a stable. Shepherds and kings come to visit. Do we know the Christmas story so well that it no longer surprises us? Or do we romanticise it in our cute nativity plays with fairylights, stars, a friendly donkey and fluffy sheep? I encourage you to read the Bible story and see:

- the scared unmarried teenager
- the fiancé wondering what to do
- the long and uncomfortable ride to Bethlehem
- the confusion over how God could allow his Son to be born among the animals
- Mary's surprise at the shepherd's visit
- Mary's wonder when the wise men turn up

Our challenge is to get across the confusion, the wonder and the excitement that are all contained within the nativity story. We want to help people realise what an enormity it really is that God came down to join us, and in the way that he did.

How does this session help people grow in Christ?

God is not remote. He came down to join us, and not as a king on a throne. He was not born in a private hospital or palace, but a lowly stable. He was conceived by an unmarried teenager and soon to become refugee. He knows what it is like to be human, to struggle and to suffer. As a result, he can understand us, support us and guide us through life. This session doesn't just tell the age-old nativity story, but tries to help people look beyond the story by raising questions at each stage.

Add value

Mealtime card
- If God came to visit today, how would he do it?
- Who are the equivalent of the shepherds today?
- Who are the equivalent of the wise men today?

Question to start and end the session
So… what surprises you most about the Christmas story?

Social action idea
Could you make some extra stars and hang them on local trees or bushes to make people smile. Make sure to use biodegradable string and ideally collect them up after Christmas to avoid litter. You could make the stars out of an advert for your Christmas service. You could also give them as presents to someone local to you who might be alone at Christmas.

Activities

1. Angel Gabriel wings

You will need: stiff white card; paper; scissors; glue; elastic; a stapler; glitter

Cut out wing shapes from the cardboard. Fold up the paper and cut feathers, several in one go. Glue them on, overlaying each other. Staple two loops of elastic in the middle for the arms. If you like glitter mess, feel free to add some! You can feather one side, or both if you have time.

Talk about how God sent an angel called Gabriel to the earth to tell Mary that she was going to give birth to God's son and to name him Jesus. He was going to be great and have a kingdom that would never end. Mary was scared but she agreed.

I wonder... how would you react if that happened to you? God can speak to us in many ways; sending angels is just one of them.

2. Road to Bethlehem – piggyback race

You will need: a blanket; cushions; a start, middle and finish line marked out; donkey ears and tails; a manger

One person (a child) puts the cushion up their jumper, holds the blanket and rides on the back of the other person (a grown up), who wears the donkey ears and tail. The donkey must carry Mary from the start line to the line in the middle, where they lie down on the blanket to 'sleep', then get up and ride onwards to the finish line. Have a manger at the finishing line to put the cushion in. If you are outside and want to add some fun, you could squirt water on them for 'rain'.

Talk about how Mary and Joseph had to travel about 90 miles from Nazareth to Bethlehem, which would have taken them days. Mary was heavily pregnant, so they may have taken a donkey. It would have been a very uncomfortable and dusty journey.

I wonder... why do you think God did not organise a fine carriage and horses for Mary and Joseph?

3. Pin the tail on the donkey

You will need: a large picture of a donkey; several tails; sticky tape or sticky tac; pens; a blindfold

Give each person a tail with their name written on it. Then blindfold them, spin them around several times and ask them to pin their tail on the donkey. The winner is the closest to the actual tail. You could extend this to bridles, backpacks, Mary and Joseph.

Talk about how donkeys were domesticated thousands of years ago and appear in the Bible many times. There is even a talking donkey! Although the nativity story does not include a donkey, Mary may well have ridden on one, and there may have been one in the stable. Jesus may even have slept in its feeding trough. We do know that 33 years later, Jesus rode on a colt (a young donkey) into Jerusalem and was cheered by a big crowd.

I wonder… have you ever ridden on a donkey? What was it like?

4. Stable

You will need: boxes; sticks; string; hay; straw; a blanket; stuffed animals, animal costumes

Build a stable. It could be out of boxes; it could be sticks tied together like fencing. Add a manger with hay. Add the animals. Lay a blanket down on some straw. Leave placing the baby for the celebration.

Talk about how God could have sent Mary and Joseph to a posh hotel or hospital, but he chose to send them to a stable.

I wonder… where were you born? Why do you think God chose for Jesus to be born in a stable?

5. Baby Jesus

You will need: sausages (veggie for food safety); ready-rolled pastry; a baking tray; baking parchment; a pen; little cardboard boxes; crisps or grated carrot

Make a swaddled baby. Cut strips of ready-rolled pastry and wrap them around the sausage, leaving a face poking out. Place him on the baking paper and write your name on the paper. Once cooked, lay him in a bed of crisps in the cardboard manger. A banana could make a sweet, sticky alternative to a sausage if you prefer.

Talk about how God could have come into this world as a mighty warrior or superstar, but he didn't. He chose to come as a tiny vulnerable baby.

I wonder… what does that say about God?

6. Shepherds sheep

You will need: green fabric to use as fake grass; cardboard tubes; shredded paper; black card; google eyes; glue; tape; scissors; black pipe cleaners

Create a hillside with the green fabric. Make sheep with cardboard tubes. Make pipe cleaner legs and a tail and push through the tube. Cut out a head and ears with a neck that can staple inside the tube. Stick on googly eyes. Stick shredded paper on to the cardboard tube (more eco-friendly than cotton wool). Place them on the 'hillside'.

Talk about how shepherds were the lowest members of society in those days. They lived outside and smelt of sheep. And yet, God invited them to be the first to see his baby son.

I wonder… why did God invite shepherds to be the first to see Jesus? How do you think Mary and Joseph reacted when they turned up? How would he want us to treat the lowest members of our societies?

7. Star

You will need: old books; old Christmas cards; old music scores; scissors; string; paper glue; coloured pens; star templates

Draw around the star template on to a page. Cut out four stars at once. Glue half of one star and half of another and stick them together. Repeat several times. Put the string through the middle before sticking the last star to the first. Use pens to colour the edges or add glitter.

Talk about how the shepherds were told to go looking for a baby in a feeding trough, but the wise men were given a star to follow. How awesome is that? God can change the stars in the heavens if he wants to, just for us. Astronomers disagree on what the Bethlehem star was. Was it a supernova, a solar flare, a comet or an alignment of planets? What do you think?

I wonder… what do you think the Bethlehem star was?

8. Treasure chest

You will need: cardboard boxes; flat cardboard; brown paint and gold paint; double-sided tape; scissors; black permanent pens

Pre-paint the boxes brown and the flat cardboard gold. Use the double-sided tape to stick on strips of gold cardboard, adding a cardboard lock and using the pen to add detail. Take it home to keep your treasures in.

Talk about when the wise men came to visit Jesus, they 'opened their treasures' and gave him gifts of gold, myrrh and frankincense. Each one had a special meaning: gold for a king, myrrh for his future sacrifice and frankincense for the priest he would become.

I wonder… what will you keep in your treasure chest? What is precious to you? Is it money or items that remind you of happy times?

9. Frankincense – potion making

You will need: small glass bottles; avocado or olive oil; gloves; dried, fragrant herbs and plants (e.g. rosemary, sage, jasmine, rose, lavender, chamomile, pine needles, cinnamon sticks, frankincense resin); a little funnel; labels; pens

Make your own perfume oil. Sprinkle different dried items into your bottle until you are happy with the smell. Then pour in the oil and shake. Write a blessing word (peace, love, joy, hope) on a sticky label and attach it to the bottle. Take the bottle home and let it sit on a sunny windowsill for three to four weeks, shaking it every week or so. Then store in a cool dark place. Use as a perfume, massage oil or to bless others.

Talk about how the wise men gave the baby Jesus frankincense, a valuable fragrant oil made from the resin of the Boswellia tree. It has been used in traditional medicine but also in religious ceremonies, burned as an offering to God. It was also used to embalm the dead.

I wonder... do you think, when they gave Jesus frankincense, the wise men knew that Jesus was God's Son or that his death would end up being so important?

10. Grab bag

You will need: cotton tote bags; paint; a sponge; brushes; card; scissors; double-sided tape; a permanent pen; cardboard; the camel template

Use the camel template to create several stencil cut-outs. Insert cardboard into the tote bag to avoid getting paint all the way through. Use a sponge to sparingly paint the background on the tote bag. Do another craft while it dries for ten minutes. Add 'GRAB BAG' in permanent pen at the top of the bag. Place the template on the edge of the bag, hold it down firmly while you sponge brown paint for the camel. Then move the template to the other edge of the bag and sponge on the person. Finally add the rope with permanent pen.

Talk about how after the wise men had gone, an angel appeared to Joseph in a dream and told him to flee to Egypt to avoid Herod's soldiers. They had to escape in the middle of the night, quickly grabbing whatever they could.

I wonder... what would you want in your grab bag for an emergency?

Celebration

Have a centrepiece of a Christmas tree with boxes of presents wrapped up, numbered 1 to 7. Inside the wrapping paper the boxes have large letters/words: I, 'M, A, MAN, WITH, U, EL. Each box contains a prop for the nativity story. Ask volunteers to unwrap the presents in order and each person takes on a role in the play. Try to get them to do simple movements to act out the story, using the giant stable you have made.

1. Angel wings (Gabriel) – Who do you think we have here? Yes, the angel Gabriel. Who has he come to see? Let's open the next present for a clue.
2. Blue scarf and cushion (Mary) – Now what could this be? The angel told Mary she was going to have a baby. Can you put the cushion up your jumper, Mary?
3. Donkey ears (Donkey) – What happened next? Where are you going to take Mary? Yes, that's right, to Bethlehem. We had better have a Joseph too. Whoever has box 4, can you be Joseph? Off you go, Donkey. Lead Mary and Joseph to our stable. Who can remember how far they had to travel? How long it took them? Yes, 90 miles in four days.
4. Doll and white cloth (Joseph) – No prizes for guessing who this is. Joseph can you wrap the newborn baby up nice and warm and place him in the manger?
5. Sheep (Shepherd) – Does anyone know what this clue is about? Yes, the shepherds came to see Jesus. How did they know where to come? The angel told them. Angel, can you show the shepherd where to find the baby? Yes, in the manger, an animal's feeding trough. Shepherd, would you like to give your sheep to the baby as a present?
6. Star (Star) – Who made a star today? Can you remember why? Yes, God put a special star in the sky to lead some special visitors to Jesus. Let's open the next box to find out who.
7. Treasure box and gifts (Wise men) – The wise men studied the stars and when they saw a new one, they knew what it meant and decided to follow it. Star, can you lead the wise men around the room? They probably took a long time. We know that the star disappeared and reappeared. They were over the moon when it finally stopped over Jesus, and they got to meet this new king and open their treasure box and give him their gifts.

Now that we have opened all the presents, can you see that each box has a letter or word on it? Let's put them down in a line and see if we can guess what they spell? I'M A MAN WITH U EL or 'I am a man with you all.'

Did you know that hundreds of years before Jesus was born, God told his prophet Isaiah this: 'A virgin will conceive and give birth to a son, and they will call him Immanuel', which means 'God with us' (*point at boxes*).

Isn't that amazing? God was planning to join us, as a human being, for hundreds of years and sent clues, so that we might recognise him when he came. He also told Isaiah that Jesus would be called: Wonderful Counsellor, Mighty God, Everlasting Father, Prince of Peace.

I wonder…
- Why didn't God provide a posh hotel for his son to be born in?
- If I had been in Mary's shoes, would I have said yes?
- What gifts would I have given to baby Jesus?

Prayer
I encourage you to gather around the stable and look at the manger as I say a short prayer. You may even like to kneel.

Wonderful Counsellor, Mighty God, Everlasting Father, Prince of Peace, thank you so much for coming down to join us here on earth. To share in our joys but also in our discomforts. Thank you that we can always come to you with our worries knowing that you understand what it is like to be human. Amen.

Song suggestions
'Come and join the celebration' – Mission Praise #83
'Away in a manger' – Mission Praise #47
'We wish you a merry Christmas' – Arthur Warrell
'Lord of the dance' (first verse and chorus) – Sydney Carter
'Do you hear what I hear' – Noël Regney

Meal suggestions
You could use Christmas cutters to make mini tree and star pizzas. You could use ready-rolled shortcrust pastry with tomato paste and grated cheese. Then add sweetcorn or olive baubles and red pepper tinsel.

Session material: January
'It's not fair!' It's all about mercy
by Becky May

 PDF DOWNLOAD    MESSY CHURCH AT HOME    MESSY CHURCH GOES WILD

Bible story for prep

John 5:1–18 (NIV)

Sometime later, Jesus went up to Jerusalem for one of the Jewish festivals. Now there is in Jerusalem near the Sheep Gate a pool, which in Aramaic is called Bethesda and which is surrounded by five covered colonnades. Here a great number of disabled people used to lie – the blind, the lame, the paralysed. One who was there had been an invalid for thirty-eight years. When Jesus saw him lying there and learned that he had been in this condition for a long time, he asked him, 'Do you want to get well?'

'Sir,' the invalid replied, 'I have no one to help me into the pool when the water is stirred. While I am trying to get in, someone else goes down ahead of me.'

Then Jesus said to him, 'Get up! Pick up your mat and walk.' At once the man was cured; he picked up his mat and walked.

The day on which this took place was a Sabbath, and so the Jewish leaders said to the man who had been healed, 'It is the Sabbath; the law forbids you to carry your mat.'

But he replied, 'The man who made me well said to me, "Pick up your mat and walk."'

So they asked him, 'Who is this fellow who told you to pick it up and walk?'

The man who was healed had no idea who it was, for Jesus had slipped away into the crowd that was there.

Later Jesus found him at the temple and said to him, 'See, you are well again. Stop sinning or something worse may happen to you.' The man went away and told the Jewish leaders that it was Jesus who had made him well.

So, because Jesus was doing these things on the Sabbath, the Jewish leaders began to persecute him. In his defence Jesus said to them, 'My Father is always at his work to this very day, and I too am working.' For this reason, they tried all the more to kill him; not only was he breaking the Sabbath, but he was even calling God his own Father, making himself equal with God.

Matthew 5:7 (NIV)

Blessed are the merciful, for they will be shown mercy.

Pointers

I was once told a definition of the word 'mercy' as 'We don't get what we deserve.' When I hear the word 'mercy', I immediately remember the game we played as children (not included here!), where you would engage in some kind of hand wrestle until a player called out 'Mercy!' It may not be a game we want to share with the next generation of children, but it does illustrate the point perfectly: the stronger player shows mercy by letting the weaker player go, ending the pain and putting an immediate stop to the activity.

The story of the man at the pool of Bethesda asks many questions: what had led him to be there? Why wouldn't anyone help him into the pool? And, perhaps more pertinent, what was his sin? This isn't a story about how a man's sin had led to his disability, and we need to be careful to make that clear, but rather that Jesus cut across the nonsense of the pool, the ill health of the man, his lonely position and saw to the heart: this man needed the mercy of Jesus. Rather than leaving the man there to wait hopelessly, Jesus intervened, showing mercy and forgiveness and a brand new, fresh start.

Download support material at **messychurch.org.uk/getmessyvol2-2878**

How does this session help people grow in Christ?

Like the man sat beside the pool, we live at a time when sometimes the wrong that we do can lead to us being ignored or 'cancelled'. John 5:1–18 shows us that Jesus saw the man, just as he sees us and treats us with mercy; not giving us what we deserve. Matthew 5:7 challenges us to be those who show mercy. When we are hurt, we cannot respond with vengeance, but are to do as Jesus did and be people who are merciful.

Add value

Mealtime card

- Can you think of a time when someone has shown you mercy?
- How do we feel when someone hurts us?
- What would it mean to show them mercy?

Question to start and end the session

So… do we always get what we deserve?

Social action idea

How can you show mercy? It may be as simple as forgiving someone who has hurt you, or it may be on a bigger scale; for example, is there a group of people in your local community who are ostracised? How can you be people of mercy to them?

Activities

1. Bubble painting

You will need: paper; large bowls of water mixed with ready-to-use poster paint and a small amount of washing up liquid; straws

Using the straw, blow into the bowl of water until a good layer of bubbles appear at the top of the bowl. Gently lay the sheet of paper on top of the bubbles to capture a print. You can experiment with using different colours and gathering the prints on the same paper so that they overlap.

Talk about how the pool that the man sat beside was said to have special powers when the water bubbled.

I wonder… why do you think people hoped that the pool would heal them? Have you ever experienced a miraculous healing? If so, share your story.

2. Go again!

You will need: board games/card games/parlour games

Set out games that are well known to the families, where you have to stop if you do something wrong, such as Jenga, pick-up sticks, Twister, etc. When the players 'fail,' say, 'It's okay, you can go again!'

Talk about how Jesus healed the man who have been an invalid for 38 years, giving him a second chance.

I wonder… how might it feel to get a second chance? How can Jesus give us a fresh start?

3. Walk through bubbles

You will need: a large container with bubble liquid or washing up liquid and water; a hula hoop ring with a strand of cotton wrapped around it (this helps the bubble liquid to stick!)

Place a hula hoop in a large container of soapy water (a tuff tray or heavy duty plastic tray is perfect for this). Experiment with creating large bubbles. Participants could remove shoes and socks and stand in the centre for the bubbles to be lifted over them.

Talk about how standing inside a bubble has a 'wow' factor. The paralysed man expected to experience something special when he went into the bubbly water but instead he experienced something even greater when Jesus spoke to him.

I wonder… how might Jesus wow us?

4. Moving man

You will need: jointed card people and split pins (wooden version available at bakerross.co.uk/wooden-person-puppet-kits); coloured pens

Put together a jointed person with the split pins then design and decorate your person; you may choose to make the figure look like the man in the story or you could follow your own moving person design. Experiment with moving your person around – can you make them walk, run and dance?

Talk about how Jesus healed the man after 38 years of not being able to move properly.

I wonder… how do you think the man might have felt when Jesus healed him? What do you think made the biggest difference to the man – that he'd been healed or that he'd been forgiven?

5. Contemplative doodling

You will need: sheets with the word 'Mercy' written in outline; colouring pens and pencils

Sit and think about what the word 'Mercy' means. As you reflect, use the pens or pencils to doodle within the outline the words, images, thoughts and feelings that come to mind.

Alternative: this could be an outdoor activity by changing it to create the word 'Mercy' out of natural objects.

Talk about how the word mercy is described as not getting what we deserve, or as showing forgiveness or compassion when it is in your power to punish or inflict pain.

I wonder… when have we experienced mercy? How does it feel to experience mercy? How does it feel to be merciful?

6. Build the colonnades

You will need: toy building bricks; junk modelling materials

Can you create a freestanding archway from the building materials provided? How long will it stand for?

Alternative: this could be an outdoor activity by using objects found in nature if taken outdoors.

Talk about how the ruin of the site of the pool of Bethesda can be found within the old city of Jerusalem. In the first century, it had five covered colonnades, which marked the site as a special place.

I wonder… why do you think this place was thought to be so special? Jesus seeing the man there made it special! Where can we meet with Jesus?

7. Carrying game

You will need: two large dolls, teddies, mannequins or scarecrows; empty paddling pool; obstacles

Arrange the players in two teams and challenge them to be the first to carry their 'person' safely through the obstacle course and into the pool. You could add extra challenges in, more difficult obstacles, or challenge teams to work in pairs, by holding hands, etc.

Talk about how the people believed that the first person in the water when the pool bubbled would be healed, but nobody would help the man in the story.

I wonder… how do you think the man may have felt when Jesus noticed him? Have you ever felt noticed? What was it like?

8. Bubble tea

You will need: a blender or smoothie maker; cooked black tapioca pearls; milk; ice cubes; soft fruits; glasses

This is a variation on the very popular bubble tea; other recipes are widely available online, including many which do include tea! Put a handful of cooked cooled tapioca pearls in the bottom of the glass, and half fill the glass with ice cubes. Using the blender, blend your chosen soft fruits and mix with milk. Pour your fruity 'tea' over the ice cubes and tapioca pearls. Enjoy!

Talk about how those who waited beside the pool wanted to be healed and have a new start. Jesus gave the man a total refresh!

I wonder… how does Jesus refresh our lives?

9. Fizzy forgiveness

You will need: Alka-Seltzer tablets; clear glasses of water

Break the Alka-Seltzer tablets in half. Drop a tablet into the water and watch as it bubbles and dissolves. As you do so, bring something to God that you want to say sorry for. As the tablet dissolves, know that God has removed that from you; it is gone and forgiven!

Talk about how it feels to know that God takes away our sin – the wrong that we do, think or say – and gives us a fresh start.

I wonder… do you need a fresh start? What gets in the way? Take some time to pray about this, either as an individual or with a trusted Christian friend.

10. Noticed!

You will need: paper; pens; access to an outdoor space; a timer

Sit and make yourself really comfortable. Using all your senses, what do you notice around you? Write a list of all the things you can hear, see, smell, taste and feel over the next three minutes. You could compare your list with other people; who is the most observant? Which sense did you rely on the most?

Talk about how the man had been ignored by the people, but Jesus noticed him.

I wonder… how does it feel to know that Jesus notices us too? What are the things and who are the people that Jesus wants us to see?

Celebration

Invite everyone to play a part in your storytelling. You will need one person to play the part of the man, and another to play the part of Jesus. You could have a few other hopeful people sat beside the pool and a busy crowd who may help those who wait. You will also need a few religious leaders, and you could have some active participants to play the part of a pool, perhaps holding ribbons or a play parachute, swirling it around and 'bubbling up'.

Today's story involves a man *(indicate this character)* who had not been able to walk for many, many years; 38 years in fact! He wanted to be well again so badly that every day he sat beside the pool at Bethesda. Now here's an interesting fact for you: Bethesda means 'house of mercy'. We've come across that word before today!

This man wasn't the only one there; in fact the pool at Bethesda was thought to be very special and have special powers, so many people who were sick or disabled *(indicate to those playing these parts)* would come near to the water in the hope that they may be healed.

The thing was, you couldn't just come near to the water, you had to go into the water. And you couldn't go into the water whenever you felt like it, nor could you go into the water altogether! The legend was that whenever the water bubbled up *(encourage those playing the part of the pool to 'bubble' the water)* only the first one into the pool would be healed!

So, the people would wait around until the water bubbled, then those in the crowd would lift someone into the water in the hope that they would be healed. But nobody would lift this man into the water. I wonder why. Perhaps he had done something wrong to upset these people? Perhaps he was grumpy or rude? Perhaps he was lonely and sad? We know he had come to this place because he wanted 'mercy'.

One day, Jesus was walking near the pool when he spotted the man and asked him if he wanted to be healed *(encourage the actors to mime)*.

'Yes!' said the man, 'but nobody will help me into the water; someone else always gets in ahead of me!'

So what do you think Jesus did? Carry him into the pool? No. Jesus stood in front of the man and said, 'Get up! Pick your mat up and walk!' And that was it! The man was healed immediately! The man didn't need a house of mercy or a pool of mercy; he needed Jesus, the God of mercy.

The man went into the town to the temple, where he showed the religious leaders what Jesus had done. When Jesus saw him there, he said something strange to him: 'Don't sin again!' Jesus had given the man a fresh start and he wanted him to use it well!

I wonder...
- How the man's life changed after this moment?
- What you have discovered about Jesus in this story?
- How it would feel to know that Jesus shows us mercy too?

Prayer
Blow bubbles over the group as you pray, perhaps using a bubble machine.

God of mercy, just as you did for the man at the bubbling pool, you take away our sin and give us the chance to start afresh. Thank you for your gift of mercy. Help us to see where we need to show mercy to others. Amen.

Song suggestions
'The bubbling pool of Bethesda' – Ishmael
'God of mercy (prayer song)' – Lou Fellingham
'His mercy is more' – Keith and Kristyn Getty

Meal suggestions
Pasta with a choice of toppings – bolognese, veggie bolognese, ham, grated cheese, tuna, etc. – followed by fresh fruit salad (use up the remaining soft fruits!)

Download support material at **messychurch.org.uk/getmessyvol2-2878**

Session material: February
What did Jesus say? 'I forgive you'
by Rachel Gotobed

 PDF **DOWNLOAD**    MESSY CHURCH **AT HOME**    MESSY CHURCH **GOES WILD**

Bible story for prep

Luke 7:36–50 (ERV)

One of the Pharisees asked Jesus to eat with him. Jesus went into the Pharisee's house and took a place at the table.

There was a sinful woman in that town. She knew that Jesus was eating at the Pharisee's house. So the woman brought some expensive perfume in an alabaster jar. She stood at Jesus' feet, crying. Then she began to wash his feet with her tears. She dried his feet with her hair. She kissed his feet many times and rubbed them with the perfume.

When the Pharisee who asked Jesus to come to his house saw this, he thought to himself, 'If this man were a prophet, he would know that the woman who is touching him is a sinner!'

In response, Jesus said to the Pharisee, 'Simon, I have something to say to you.'

Simon said, 'Let me hear it, Teacher.'

Jesus said, 'There were two men. Both men owed money to the same banker. One man owed him 500 silver coins. The other man owed him 50 silver coins. The men had no money, so they could not pay their debt. But the banker told the men that they did not have to pay him. Which one of those two men will love him more?'

Simon answered, 'I think it would be the one who owed him the most money.'

Jesus said to him, 'You are right.' Then he turned to the woman and said to Simon, 'Do you see this woman? When I came into your house, you gave me no water for my feet. But she washed my feet with her tears and dried my feet with her hair. You did not greet me with a kiss, but she has been kissing my feet since I came in. You did not honour me with oil for my head, but she rubbed my feet with her sweet-smelling oil. I tell you that her many sins are forgiven. This is clear, because she showed great love. People who are forgiven only a little will love only a little.'

Then Jesus said to her, 'Your sins are forgiven.'

The people sitting at the table began to think to themselves, 'Who does this man think he is? How can he forgive sins?'

Jesus said to the woman, 'Because you believed, you are saved from your sins. Go in peace.'

Pointers

There are many stories in the gospels that show how Jesus offers forgiveness, and sometimes they are accompanied by him telling a parable to help us understand how and why we should be willing to forgive too. Ultimately, we know that it is because of his death and resurrection that our sins are forgiven, because he willingly sacrificed his life for us. But as recipients of his forgiveness, he asks us to forgive others, and we don't always find that easy.

Forgiveness can be a messy business! People feel hurt over all sorts of situations, and even when an apology has been offered, sometimes we hear them say things like, 'That is unforgivable!' However, in teaching his followers to pray, Jesus includes the lines, 'Forgive our sins, just as we have forgiven those who did wrong to us' (Matthew 6:12), and he also says, 'Don't judge others, and God will not judge you. Don't condemn others, and you will not be condemned. Forgive others, and you will be forgiven' (Luke 6:37).

In the story, Jesus asks the Pharisee who has invited him for dinner to interpret the parable he told, to try to help the Pharisee understand the forgiveness Jesus affords us all, including the woman the Pharisee calls sinful. Jesus' forgiveness is not like our natural inclination to only forgive as we feel is justified, but rather it is a forgiveness for all, and of all, and he wants us to forgive others this way too.

Photocopying not permitted except under the CLA Church Licence.

How does this session help people grow in Christ?

Forgiveness is a fundamental part of the gift of salvation offered by God, in Christ, to us all. We read in 1 John 1:9: 'But God is faithful and fair. If we confess our sins, he will forgive our sins. He will forgive every wrong thing we have done. He will make us pure' (NIRV). Having heard him say, 'I forgive you,' we cannot simply accept this great gift and not be changed by it. Rather it is such forgiveness, and a total surrender of our lives, that starts us on a lifelong journey of transformation by the Holy Spirit.

Add value

Mealtime card
- Have you ever been invited somewhere special for dinner?
- Do you have a favourite smell or perfume/aftershave?
- How easy do you find it to forgive someone?
- What does it feel like to know Jesus forgives you?

Question to start and end the session
So… how can we know that Jesus forgives us, and how can we be forgiving towards others?

Social action idea
Ephesians 4:32 says: 'Be kind and compassionate to one another, forgiving each other, just as in Christ God forgave you' (NIV). Can you think of some ways that you could show kindness towards someone who isn't always kind to others, either at school or in your neighbourhood? Alternatively, some cafes do a 'Pay it forward' scheme so you can buy an extra drink that can be given to someone in need.

Activities

1. Potpourri/lavender bags

You will need: potpourri or dried lavender; material; a circular template (20 cm); scissors; elastic band; ribbon. Alternatively you could use premade organza bags.

Cut out a circle of material using the template provided. Add a tablespoon of potpourri/lavender in the centre of the material and gather it together to make a pouch. Use the elastic band to secure the pouch shut and then tie a piece of ribbon around it. If using premade organza bags, you could use gems or sequins to stick on them.

Talk about how the woman in the story poured perfume on Jesus' feet when he was having dinner.

I wonder… why do you think she did that? What do you do to make people feel welcome when they visit?

2. Foot washing

You will need: bowls of warm water; soap; flannels; towels

Have bowls of warm water and soap available for people to wash their feet or someone else's. This could work well set up next to foot painting (Activity 3)!

Talk about how it was the custom at the time of Jesus to have your feet washed. Can you guess why? What other Bible stories mention foot washing?

I wonder… how did it feel to have your feet washed? Have you ever been anywhere where you were offered to have your feet washed on arrival? What was it like to wash someone else's feet?

3. Foot painting

You will need: washable paint; perfume; spices or vanilla extract; paper; paintbrushes; pens

Mix perfume, spices or vanilla extract in washable paint. Spread a thin layer of the paint on the soles of your feet and print footprint pictures. Write on the top of the paper, 'Jesus says, "I forgive you"', and then add your name at the bottom.

Talk about how the woman in the story shows Jesus how much she loves him by washing his feet with her tears, drying them with her hair and then pouring expensive perfume on them.

I wonder… how can we show Jesus that we love him?

4. Anointing oil

You will need: small bottles with lids or droppers; olive oil; essential oil (e.g. frankincense or lavender); teaspoons; funnels; droppers

Make a small bottle of anointing oil using two drops of essential oil to one teaspoon of olive oil.

Talk about how anointing oil in the Bible is used to symbolise God's power, presence, healing, consecration and hospitality. It is also used as a way of showing love and respect for others, just like the woman putting perfume on Jesus' feet in the story.

I wonder… what can we do to show love and respect for others?

Download support material at **messychurch.org.uk/getmessyvol2-2878**

5. It's a wrap!

You will need: small flour tortillas; selection of fillings, including cream cheese, grated cheese, cold meats, lettuce, peppers, cucumber, tomatoes, etc.; plates; knives

Make sandwich wraps using the ingredients provided. Be aware of food allergies and have vegan and gluten-free options available.

Talk about how we are not told in the story what was on the menu when Jesus went to dinner at the Pharisee's house. What do you think they may have had?

I wonder… what would you prepare to eat if Jesus were coming to dinner?

6. Coin counting challenge

You will need: bags of 100 two-pence coins; stopwatch; paper; pen

Time each participant as they count the bag of coins into ten stacks of ten coins. Keep a leader board of times to see who does it the quickest.

Talk about the parable Jesus told at the Pharisee's house about two people who owed money – one owed 500 coins and the other 50. At the time of the story, one coin would have been the average pay for one day's work. Talk about how the moneylender forgave their debts and cancelled what they owed.

I wonder… which person will love the moneylender more in Jesus' story?

7. Love you cards

You will need: red or pink card; foil-covered chocolate hearts; glue dots; pens; scissors

Cut out a heart shape from the card and using a glue dot, stick a foil-covered chocolate heart in the centre. Write at the top, 'God loves you' and underneath, 'and I do too!' You can write a personal message on the back and then give the card to someone you love.

Talk about St Valentine's Day (14 February) traditionally is a special day set aside to tell people we love them; however, we can do this every day! In the story, the woman shows how much she loves Jesus by pouring perfume over his feet.

I wonder… how do you show love for Jesus?

8. Wiping away our sins

You will need: A4 whiteboards or laminated sheets of paper; whiteboard (washable) markers; wet wipes

Write a prayer asking Jesus to forgive you for the wrong things you have done. When you have prayed your prayer, wipe the words away knowing that Jesus says, 'I forgive you.'

Talk about how the Bible uses the word 'sin' to describe the wrong things we do. In the story, Jesus forgives the woman of her sins. 1 John 1:9 tells us: 'But God is faithful and fair. If we confess our sins, he will forgive our sins. He will forgive every wrong thing we have done. He will make us pure' (NIRV).

I wonder... is there something we need forgiveness for? Find a quiet space and see what thoughts God puts in your head. Chat with God about this and ask for his forgiveness.

9. Woven placemats

You will need: one piece of A4 paper or card; strips of coloured paper approximately 30 cm long and 2 cm wide; scissors; sticky tape

Hold the A4 piece of paper landscape and fold it in half. Cut slits along the fold starting approximately 2 cm from the edge and 2 cm apart. Unfold the paper and weave the coloured paper strips in and out of the slits and secure the ends with sticky tape.

Talk about whether you have a set of table mats at home? What pictures are on them? Do you have any for special occasions, such as Christmas? Do you think the Pharisee may have got the best mats and plates out when he invited Jesus to dinner?

I wonder... what preparations might you make if you were inviting Jesus over for dinner?

10. Tea tasting

You will need: a variety of fruit teas that have been made and cooled; jugs; cups

Try to guess what kind of tea it is, first by smelling it and then by tasting it. You could do it blindfolded.

Talk about how some things are recognisable by their taste and smell. How easy was it to guess the different kinds of teas? Was it easier by smell or taste?

I wonder... what the house smelt like when the woman poured perfume on Jesus' feet?

Celebration

Start by watching an animated version of the story found in Luke 7:36–50, such as those produced by Saddleback Kids on YouTube.

Ask for three volunteers and get them to help you retell the parable found in today's story (Luke 7:41–42) of the two people who borrowed money from the lender. Have some bags of chocolate coins to illustrate the difference in the amounts loaned, and ask the same question as Jesus did, 'Which one of them will love him (the moneylender) more?' You do not need 550 coins – you can just have 1 large bag and 1 small bag.

The story tells us that the woman who brought the perfume and washed Jesus' feet had done many wrong things, but by showing her love for him in this way, Jesus forgave her and told her to 'go in peace' (v. 50). All of us do wrong things, which the Bible calls sin, and because God is holy and pure, our sins separate us from him. However, God loves us all so much, he sent his only Son, Jesus, to die for us so that we can be forgiven (John 3:16), and when we say sorry to him, he says, 'I forgive you.'

The Bible teaches us a lot about forgiveness – not only about how we can be forgive, but also about how we should be willing to forgive others. Most of us don't always find this easy, especially if we have been very hurt, but in teaching his followers to pray, Jesus includes the lines, 'Forgive our sins, just as we have forgiven those who did wrong to us' (Matthew 6:12), and he also says, 'Forgive others, and you will be forgiven' (Luke 6:37).

Share out the chocolate coins used to retell the parable, making sure everyone has one. (Be aware of allergies and give an alternative if necessary.) Tell people to carefully unwrap the coin and let them eat the chocolate. Then, get them to use the foil to make a heart shape to represent their love for God and for others. As you sing a song or play some music, invite people to come forward to place their heart shape foil around a cross as a sign that they are sorry for their sins and to show their love.

I wonder...
- How the woman felt when Jesus said, 'Your sins are forgiven'?
- What the perfume smelled like?
- How Simon the Pharisee felt after his dinner with Jesus?

Prayer
Say the Lord's Prayer as a group. Don't presume that everyone will know it, so have it on the screen and/or on a take-home card. You could suggest that people use the prayer at home over the coming month.

You could teach the actions as illustrated in the Messy Church video at **youtu.be/tOugEQpcc_k**. *Or if you want a multicultural version of the Lord's Prayer see* **youtu.be/BreKg1W5S_s**.

Song suggestions
'God's love is big, God's love is great' – Vineyard Worship
'Thank you for every new good morning' – S. Lonsdale and Michael A. Baughen
'Friend of God' – Israel Houghton
'Freely, freely' – Carol Owens

Meal suggestions
You could use the sandwich wraps made in the activities above with a bag of crisps. Alternatively, you could make something that has a distinctive aroma, such as a curry or fish and chips.

Additional copies can be purchased at **brfonline.org.uk/new-get-messy** or using the order form on page 72.

Session material: March
All can be saved
by Arul Israel and Karen Ashton

 PDF DOWNLOAD  MESSY CHURCH AT HOME  MESSY CHURCH GOES WILD

Bible story for prep

John 3:16–17 (NLV)

For God so loved the world that he gave his only Son. Whoever puts his trust in God's Son will not be lost but will have life that lasts forever. For God did not send his Son into the world to say it is guilty. He sent his Son so the world might be saved from the punishment of sin by him.

Acts 10:9–16 (NLV)

The next day they went on their way. About noon they were coming near the town. At this time Peter went up on the roof to pray. He became very hungry and wanted something to eat. While they were getting food ready to eat, he saw in a dream things God wanted him to see. He saw heaven open up and something like a large linen cloth being let down to earth by the four corners. On the cloth were all kinds of four-footed animals and snakes of the earth and birds of the sky. A voice came to him, 'Get up, Peter, kill something and eat it.' Peter said, 'No, Lord! I have never eaten anything that our Law says is unclean.' The voice said the second time, 'What God has made clean you must not say is unclean.' This happened three times. Then it was taken back to heaven.

Pointers

In Acts 10, Peter gets a vision which makes him realise that he shouldn't judge anything or anyone of God's creation as impure or unclean. Many years later John Wesley (one of the founders of Methodism) said: 'All need to be saved. All may be saved. All may know themselves saved. All may be saved to the uttermost.'

Instead of being saved by rituals or law or custom, the extract from John shows us how we are all saved.

How does this session help people grow in Christ?

This session helps us become more aware of God's love for everyone: those who are lost, have success or failure, those who let themselves or others down, those who are troubled or at peace, those who have everything or have nothing. It helps everyone to think about the diversity of God's creation and about being more welcoming without any judgements. It encourages listening and noticing messages from God.

Add value

Mealtime card
- What's your biggest challenge at the moment?
- What challenges might you face when meeting people for the first time?
- Why do you think God lets us face challenges in life?
- What do you think you would do if you were invited to go with new people you have just met? How do you know it is safe?

Question to start and end the session
So… who will be saved?

Social action idea
You could host an inclusive cafe that welcomes all (Is it accessible? Is there a quiet corner?), including new people, showing generous hospitality.

Before the next Messy Church, have a face-to-face conversation with at least five different people, including one new person, one with different interests and one you may find difficult to chat with.

Keep an open mind when meeting someone new. Remember they are a precious gift from God! How does this change your pre-conceived ideas or judgements?

Activities

1. Following a trail

You will need: a trail or labyrinth that fits your surroundings – if outdoors, consider using natural materials to lay a trail (such as pebbles or sticks); a map; numbered stations; story prompts to reflect on along the path

Create a trail or labyrinth to represent Peter's journey. Link it with a map and have numbered stations that link to the various activities with the story. Participants can wonder as they journey.

Talk about what Peter found out on his journey? I wonder how he felt (as a Jew) knowing that he was going against the law to visit someone he shouldn't (a non-Jew)?

I wonder... how would it feel to meet an angel/have a vision?

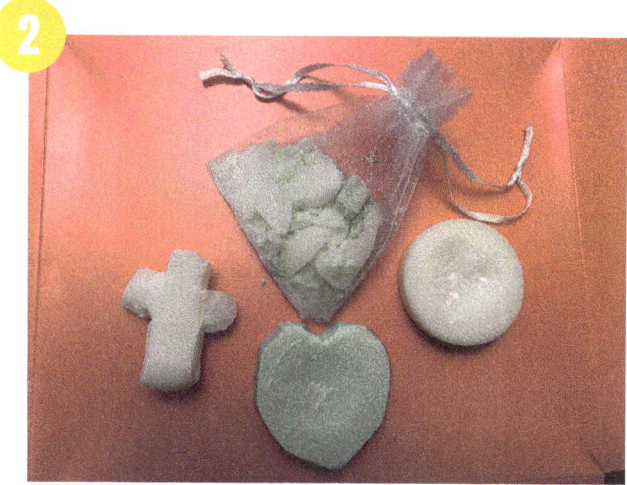

2. Soap carving

You will need: bars of soap; tools to either carve or scratch patterns into it (depending on the age range of participants)

Choose a shape – either a heart or a cross – and either carve the soap into that shape (by carefully cutting away parts of the bar) or scratch that shape into the top of the soap bar.

(Tip: collet up all the soap fragments and put them in a net bag to be used to wash hands. You could leave a note up about where these soap fragments came from and advertise the next Messy Church.)

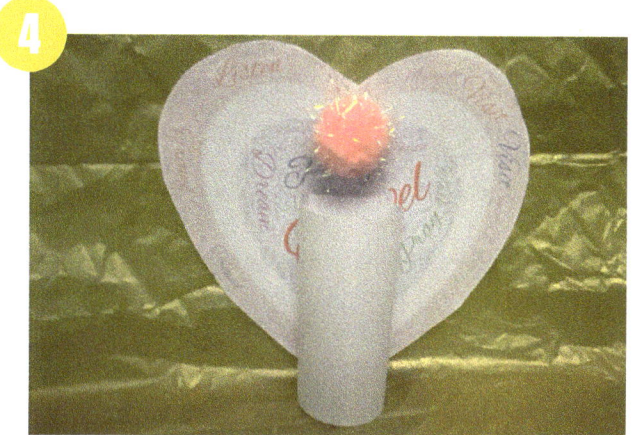

Talk about what soap physically does to our hands when we wash them. The Bible tells us that we are cleansed of our sins (the things we do wrong) by the cross (for soap crosses) and by the love of God (for hearts). The cross offers salvation, and Jesus loves all of us.

I wonder... what do I need to say sorry to God about?

3. Cleansing

You will need: dirty toys/objects; washing up bowls with clean soapy water; 'walking trays'; soil; towels to dry obejects or feet

This one can be as messy as you have space/facilities for. Whatever you choose, start with something dirty and clean it. For example, dirty toys or objects for people to clean or have trays filled with soil for people to walk through and then have bowls of warm soapy water to clean the dirt off.

Talk about what it's like to play with dirty toys? How did it feel to know that they can be cleaned? What was it like to clean the dirty toy/objects? What helped to clean the objects?

I wonder... how do you think God helps us to become clean on the inside (our thoughts and feelings) as well as on the outside (our visible actions)?

4. Angels can appear at any time – not just Christmas

You will need: heart-shape templates (see template); a printer; card paper to print on; toilet roll (or create a tube using a card); pom-pom balls in various colours (include multiple skin colours); glue or double-sided tape; pens; scissors

Print the heart-shape template on cards. To make an angel, cut out the given heart template that carries the messages that appear in the story (Acts 10). Leave the tip of the heart attached to both heart shapes so that it can be folded at that point. In the template provided, we used: travel, dream, pray, journey, talk, visit, listen and message. You can add more of your own words. Attach your heart to the tube and add a pom-pom head.

Talk about whether you knew that God uses angels as messengers throughout the Bible – they don't just appear at Christmas. What do you think it would be like to see an angel or hear a message from them? Talk about the fact that it is okay to be amazed, scared, excited or a bit disbelieving, but that it would be good to listen and try to understand what God is telling you.

I wonder... what would you do if an angel appeared to you?

5. Biscuit decorating

You will need: baked (or bought) heart-shaped biscuits; icing (ideally in at least two colours to give choice); multicoloured sprinkles (e.g. hundreds and thousands)

Decorate a biscuit to show that we should love all sorts of people (represented by the multiple colours and shapes of sprinkles). If heart-shaped biscuits are not available, use writing icing to draw a heart and fill in with icing.

Talk about how we are all different, e.g. skin colours, culture, accents, languages, but we are all loved by God. What do you think is similar about you and the person next to you? And what is different between you both? How do you feel about your similarities and differences?

I wonder... what do you think about God loving everyone despite the differences? Who do you find harder to love? For older groups, use the phrases of 'equality, diversity and inclusion' and reference the resources from your context (e.g. for Methodism – **methodist.org.uk/about-us/the-methodist-church/the-inclusive-methodist-church/training-for-justice-dignity-and-solidarity/edi-toolkit-equality-diversity-and-inclusion**).

6. The great mural

You will need: a large area of wall (inside or out) that you can cover with paper for painting or drawing on, or a large notice board with plain backing paper; various colours of paint diluted with water and poured into many empty cleaned spraying bottles, or marker pens in various colours

Paint or draw a mural. Notice how all of us bring different creative beauty to this art and we need each other, tall and short, to reach some parts of the large wall. Celebrate the diversity of God's creation of us and bringing together joyous creativity from all participants.

Talk about what is challenging about doing this mural together? What is the best thing about doing this art together?

I wonder... how did making this mural art together make you feel?

7. Quiet sensory space

You will need: a 'Quiet corner' sign; sensory items, such as headphones with calming music/ear defenders, fidget spinners, liquid motion timers, aqua lamps; suitable books; a Bible; plain paper; colouring pencils; mindful colouring sheets; squidgy toys; LED dimmed lights; a variety of fabrics of different colours and texture, such as chiffon, nets, velvet, silk; a variety of lovely smelling little drawers of surprises, such as cinnamon, flowers, soap

Set up a suitable quiet corner with a tent or a den or a sensory room. Have soft calming music in the room or have headphones available. Encourage both adults and children to lie down in this quiet space and 'Chat and catch' with God. What would you like to say to God? Chat to God about it and see if you can catch God's reply. You might want to draw a response. Find out more about 'chat and catch' from Parenting for Faith: **parentingforfaith.org.uk/tool/chat-and-catch**

Talk about how in Acts 10, Peter heard a message from God through an angel and through a vision. Explore with everyone the different ways people catch God's voice. It's unusual to hear a voice out loud. It might be a thought, a feeling, a mental picture, a wise word from someone else or a Bible verse.

I wonder... how do you hear God's messages to you?

8. Seeing messages

You will need: wax crayons; watery paint; card; Bible messages

Use wax crayons (white crayon on white card works well) to write some words or messages. The messages can be revealed by using watery coloured paint. Give everyone a message to reveal (and keep) and ask them to write one for someone with the paint (If the paper is too thin, it sometimes isn't as clear; old dividers/thin card works well.) Messages could be from Acts 10 or a mix of Bible verses and messages on various shapes.

Talk about how sometimes we don't always see the important messages that God is giving to us. Have you ever received an encouraging message from a friend? Were you surprised with what they asked you to do?

I wonder… do you have a story to share about receiving a message from God?

9. Parachute games

You will need: either a parachute or a sheet; lots of toy animals (soft ones are better) or multicoloured balls. If using animals, try to get some of those that Peter might have seen in his vision in Acts 10:12.

Play games with the parachute and sheet. Some games can be played just with the parachute. Get everyone to stand around the edge and hold on to the parachute. Practice lifting it up and down as a group. Give everyone an animal group, choosing maybe four categories: lion, snake, parrot, horse. As you lift the parachute, call out an animal group and get them to swap places while it is raised in the air. Then call out two animal groups and get them to swap places, etc. If you have balls or animals you can slowly lift and lower the parachute to make them move around and get all mixed up.

Talk about Peter's vision of a sheet with all four-legged animals, reptiles and birds in Acts 10:12 – how he saw animals that were 'unclean' according to his laws and traditions, but that he heard a message saying it was okay to eat them. Discuss about times when society or laws have said that certain people are not as good as others (e.g. Apartheid, segregation in the USA, the Troubles in Northern Ireland) and remember that still today in some place's laws need changing to give everyone equality. For younger people, think about 'rules' and what is 'fair'.

I wonder… what is God challenging you about?

10. Creating a welcoming home

You will need: junk modelling, Lego or wooden building blocks. If you have a large enough space, you might create larger models from bigger delivery boxes. If you want something that can be taken away, use cereal or shoe boxes.

Build a model of a house of welcome – it could be where you live or anywhere you feel at home.

Talk about how important (but sometimes hard) it is to welcome people who are different to us into our houses. Think about what you do to make guests feel welcome: show them round (where's the toilet!), let them rest after a journey, feed them, entertain them, listen to their stories?

I wonder… how might you welcome a visitor from a different land to your Messy Church? What might be needed; for example, different foods, a blanket or coat if they have come from a hot place and your home is colder? What else can you think of?

Celebration

You will need: volunteers representing/dressed up as an angel, Cornelius, two servants, a Roman soldier and Peter.

We are going to learn about a centurion (a commander of 100 Roman soldiers), Cornelius (Acts 10). Cornelius was a centurion in the Roman army soon after Jesus died, and this is what he learned. He was a good man who believed in God. He and his family were generous to people and regularly prayed to God. One day an angel came to Cornelius in a vision. The angel told him to send for the apostle Peter, who was living in Joppa. The angel said that Peter would tell Cornelius what to do. The next day, Cornelius sent two servants and a soldier to bring Peter to him.

Continue the story using the 'Telling the story' section fom the BRF Ministries website **brf.org.uk/product/peter-and-cornelius.**

Peter lived in Joppa. He was praying while waiting for food to be ready, he was very hungry and then fell asleep. (Ask Peter to sit in the middle of a circle made by the others and lie down, pretending to be asleep. On the signal of a clap from you – the leader – Peter should wake up still dreaming and rub his stomach to indicate that he is very hungry. Now invite three members of the circle to go over to him and suggest some unusual, exotic foods to eat.)

Each time, **Peter** should say: **'I couldn't possibly eat that'.**

To which **everyone in the circle** should reply: **'But, Peter, God made all these foods and says they're okay.'**

Now stamp your foot on the floor to imitate the banging on a door and announce that there are three visitors.

Members of the circle say together: 'Go with the visitors'.

Visitors say to Peter: 'Our master, Cornelius, would like you to come to his house to meet him'.

Peter: 'I couldn't possibly meet your master. It's against the law for someone like me to meet a Gentile.'

To which **everyone in the circle** replies: 'But, Peter, God made all these people and says they're okay. Go! Meet Cornelius.'

While Peter travels with the three visitors, questions below can be read to wonder.

Peter arrives at the centurion's house. Peter meets not only Cornelius but also his family and friends. Cornelius told Peter about the angel and said, 'We are all here before God, to hear all things that you have been commanded to tell us.'

I wonder...
- Why was Peter unwilling to eat the different animals he saw in his vision?
- Why did God need to prepare Peter so carefully (such as by sending the vision three times) before he met Cornelius?
- Why do you think the Jews didn't mix with Romans?
- What do you think Peter was thinking about as he travelled to see Cornelius?
- What do you think Peter's friends thought of what he was doing?
- What Cornelius discovers in this story?
- What is our role in God's plan to save everyone?

Prayer
Provide a pack of multicoloured sweets – for example, a mini pack of Skittles. Talk about how, even though there are different colours, each one tastes just as nice as the others. You can print the prayer on a card to go with each packet. Use the different coloured sweets as prompts to pray:

Green   *Give thanks... for something or someone.*

Red   *Ask for help... to share God's love with everyone.*

Yellow   *Reflect... God loves all of us. Let us be open minded when we meet new people and those who are different to us, step out of our comfort zone and begin conversation to get to know individuals.*

Orange   *Say sorry... for times when we are unfriendly and unkind to those who we meet or know, especially people who are different to us.*

Purple   *Decide... to see each person as made in the image of God and they are loved. Show unconditional generosity and kindness.*

Song suggestions
'God so loved' – Heart of God Church
'Lord, I lift your name on high' – Maranatha! Music
'I cannot tell why he, whom angels worship' – Mission Praise #266
'Lord of the dance' – Sydney Carter

Meal suggestions
Following the theme of diversity, serve various types of pasta (penne, fusilli, conchiglie, farfalle, etc.) to resonate that though they look different, they are each just as nourishing and tasty as each other shape. Have a variety of toppings available, such as basil and tomato, cheese, minced meat in tomato sauce, served with different types of bread. For dessert you can have animal-shaped biscuits (buy or bake them) and animal-themed 'safari' yoghurt tubes – to remember Peter's vision with all the different animal species.

Session material: April
Jesus cares for us: Jesus' last meal with his friends
by Johannah Myers and Jillian Mayer

 PDF DOWNLOAD    MESSY CHURCH AT HOME    MESSY CHURCH GOES WILD

Bible story for prep

John 13—17 (CEB)

Before the Festival of Passover, Jesus knew that his time had come to leave this world and go to the Father. Having loved his own who were in the world, he loved them fully.

John 13:1

Pointers

Experiment with your sugar scrub 'formula' ahead of time. Find a mix of oil and sugar that works best for you.

Decide ahead of time how you will use the care kits. Will folks take them home to distribute individually or will you collect them for a specific organisation?

How does this session help people grow in Christ?

Does Jesus love us and care for us? Yes, of course! But what does that love and care look like? In Jesus' last meal with his friends (disciples), Jesus shows us what that care looks like. Jesus washes his disciples' feet (that his, he serves them). Jesus teaches them more about what they need to know as he departs. And Jesus prays for them. These are examples of how Jesus loves us. During this meal, Jesus says that those who love him love others. How do we love others? We follow Jesus' example – we serve, we teach and we pray for others.

Add value

Mealtime card
- When did you last help/serve someone? When was the last time someone served you?
- Who is/has been your favourite teacher? What made them so terrific?
- Have you ever taught someone? Who did you teach? What did you teach them?

Question to start and end the session
So… what are the ways Jesus shows his love for us?

Social action idea
Use the care kit activity to encourage Messy friends to support those in need in your community or beyond. How many care kits can you make together? Invite others, even from your 'traditional' church, to donate items for the care kit.

Make the sugar scrub and bottle it in nice containers. Could you sell the sugar scrubs you make and donate the money to an organisation in your community that helps others?

Activities

1. Sugar scrub

You will need: coconut oil (grapeseed or other types of oil will work, too, including baby oil); sugar (cane sugar works well); small jars/containers; bowls; spoons; tags for jars; essential oils (optional)

To make the sugar scrub, start with a 2:1 ratio of oil to sugar and adjust as needed. Coconut oil needs to be room temperature or warm enough to stir in (doesn't have to be melted). Use essential oils carefully and only add a small amount at a time. Mix together in a bowl and then fill the jars. Add a label to the jar.

To use the sugar scrub, simply put a small amount of the scrub in your hand and rub in. Wash off and enjoy smooth, soft skin!

Ask for donations of jars or containers ahead of time; they need to have a good lid. These jars of sugar scrub could be given away as gifts. Add a small ribbon to the lid with the label to make it extra special.

Talk about how walking around in dust and dirt would have made the disciples' feet dry and dirty. Imagine how wonderful it would feel to have someone wash your feet, caring for you this way. As you use the sugar scrub, imagine how much Jesus loves and cares for you!

I wonder... whose feet are you willing to wash?

2. Care kits

You will need: items for making care kits (e.g. lip balm, lotion, sunscreen, baby wipes, band aids/plasters, simple food such as beef jerky or trail mix, socks, gloves); bags to put items in; notecards; markers

Ahead of time, decide who will receive the care kits. Will folks take them home to hand out to the homeless? Will you give these to a specific charity? Once you've decided this, you can decide what items need to go in your kit.

Have folks fill the bags with items. Make a card that says 'You matter' to include in the bag. You may have to omit this card if you are sending the items to a specific charity, depending on their rules. For US-based Messy Churches or those within the Methodist Connection (or beyond), one possibility for bags may be the hygiene kits for the United Methodist Committee on Relief. Read more about those at: **umcmission.org/umcor-hygiene-kit**.

Talk about how in the time of Jesus, people wore sandals or other types of shoes that wouldn't have kept feet clean from dirt or dust. Washing people's feet and caring for those most basic needs would have been an act of kindness and a sign of hospitality often offered by hosts or the host's servants. Jesus washed his disciples' feet as a sign of love.

I wonder... what acts of kindness, hospitality and love can we offer in our community?

3. Jesus teaches: 'I am the way' maze

You will need: yarn; a cross (or other symbol of Jesus); obstacles/objects to create a maze

Create a maze for participants to navigate using the string. You'll want one string to lead to the end of the maze where the cross is. You'll also want to create several decoy strings that do not lead to the cross.

To begin, participants should select a string and follow it with the goal of ending up at the cross. They should follow their selected line, leaving it as it is so that others can try it. If they reach a dead-end, participants can go back to the start and select a new string to start with.

Talk about how in today's scripture, Thomas asked an age-old question, 'How can we know the way?' Jesus' response was: 'I am the way, the truth and the life, no one comes to the Father except through me.' Sometimes it can be hard to know the way forward. When you're faced with a choice of a path to take, it can be really difficult to know which way to go. Luckily, as Christians we know someone who can help us to make the right choices: Jesus. Next time you're not sure what decision to make, ask him to help you do the right thing.

I wonder... where do you need God's direction in your life?

4. Erupting flour paint

You will need: water; flour; bicarbonate of soda; food colouring or liquid watercolour paint; vinegar; spray bottles; heavy paper; paint brushes; bowls/containers for paint

Add 2 tablespoons of flour to 1 tablespoon of bicarbonate of soda. Add in food colouring or liquid watercolour and water a little at a time until mixture reaches a paint-like consistency. (Don't add too much water or it messes up the paper.)

Paint your masterpiece with the flour paint.

When you're finished painting, use a spray bottle filled with vinegar to spray your painting. Watch how the paint bubbles and spreads. Note – you may need to add more bicarb for a better effect; a 1:1 ratio of flour to bicarb may be better.

Talk about what happened when we added the vinegar to the paint? Jesus said he was leaving his disciples with peace, joy and love. As friends of Jesus, we're called to spread peace, joy and love into the world like Jesus.

I wonder... what are ways we can bubble over with peace, joy and love?

5. A jar of prayers

You will need: jars or cans, enough for each attendee to have their own (this is a great opportunity to upcycle mismatched jars); decorating supplies (ribbon, glass markers, washi tape, paint); permanent markers; craft sticks (at least seven per participant)

Pick out a jar and decorate it as you like, making sure to label it as a prayer jar. Write your name on seven craft sticks and leave them at the station for others to add to

Download support material at **messychurch.org.uk/getmessyvol2-2878**

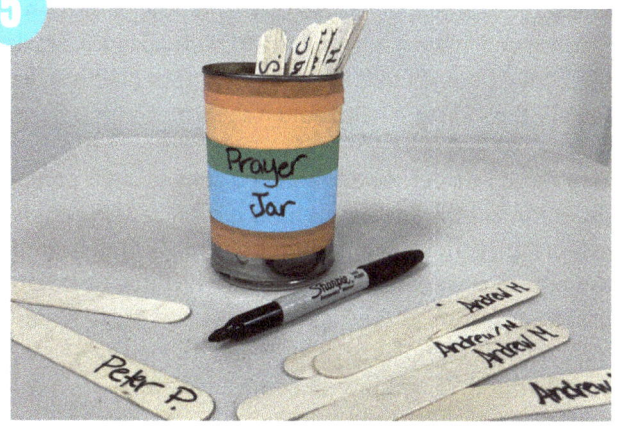

their own prayer jar. Add at least seven crafts sticks with the names of other Messy Church participants to your own prayer jar. Take your jar home and place it in a prominent place so you remember to pray for your Messy Church family.

Talk about how Jesus prayed for his disciples (John 17:11 – 'Holy Father, watch over them in your name, the name you gave me, that they will be one just as we are one.') Likewise, we should pray for our Messy Church family.

I wonder… who or what situation needs your prayers?

6. Foot-washing station

You will need: bowls or basins; water; dish soap; rags or sponges; non-porous dolls (e.g. Barbie dolls)

Choose a doll and wash its feet by dipping a rag in soapy water and rubbing them. Alternatively, offer to wash someone else's feet.

Talk about how Jesus chose to wash his disciples' feet and taught us all a lesson in humility. To wash a person's foot is to literally lower yourself before them. When Jesus was alive, the task of washing feet would have been quite a dirty one (imagine how dirty your feet would be if you were walking in sandals on the roads of Jerusalem) and one that likely only a servant would do. By washing his disciples' feet, Jesus showed a selfless, humble love.

I wonder… what are ways that you can show love and humility like Jesus?

7. Parable writing

You will need: lined paper; pens/pencils; examples of parables, such as: the yeast (Matthew 13:33), the good Samaritan (Luke 10:25–37), the soils (Matthew 13:3–9)

Try writing a parable by following these steps:
1 Pick a moral lesson you'd like to cover (e.g. show love and kindness)
2 Consider the consequences (e.g. what might happen if the lesson is not followed? What if it is?)
3 Write a beginning, middle and end. The beginning should set the stage and tell us who all the main characters are, while establishing important themes; in the middle, some kind of problem or conflict emerges; and in the end, we learn about the results of that conflict or how the story concludes.

An example of a parable: In a quiet town, there was a little cat named Luna. Luna was known for her graceful charm and soft, velvet fur. She wandered the streets, visiting homes and shops, and was welcomed by everyone for her friendly disposition.

One day, Luna was exploring near a bakery, and she met a grumpy old baker named Mr Higgins. Mr Higgins was often short-tempered and had a reputation for being unfriendly. Luna, however, paid no attention to his gruff demeanour and approached him with a gentle purr, rubbing her head against his leg.

Mr Higgins, surprised by Luna's affection, couldn't help but smile. He reached down to pet her and soon found himself talking to the little cat. Luna continued to visit the bakery regularly, always showing kindness to Mr Higgins, even when he was at his grumpiest.

Over time, Luna's visits had a profound effect on Mr Higgins. He began to soften, his frown turned into a smile more often, and he became more pleasant to his customers. People noticed the change in him and were amazed at how Luna, a simple cat, had transformed the grumpy baker.

One day, a curious customer asked Mr Higgins, 'What's made you so cheerful lately?'

Mr Higgins thought for a moment and then gestured to Luna, who was purring contentedly in the corner. He replied, 'It's this little cat, Luna. She taught me that kindness can melt even the hardest of hearts. She treated me with love and warmth, even when I didn't deserve it.'

Word spread throughout the town about Luna's remarkable ability to bring out the best in people through kindness. The townsfolk began to treat one another with more kindness and patience, just as Luna had done with Mr Higgins.

And so, the town changed for the better, all because of a little cat named Luna who taught them that treating everyone with kindness, regardless of their disposition, could bring about positive transformation in the lives of those around them. Luna's simple act of love and gentleness had shown that even the most unlikable of individuals could be touched by kindness, ultimately making the world a brighter and more compassionate place.

Talk about when Jesus spoke to the crowds he often spoke in parables, he shared stories to express symbolically who and what God and his kingdom are like. A lot of the time, people didn't completely understand what he was trying to say. Often the parables were shocking to them. These simple, shocking stories stuck with people. They were hard to forget. They almost always shattered some kind of misconception about the world, God and how we should act towards one another.

I wonder... what parable will you write? Or what parable could you rewrite for today's context?

8. Flatbread making

You will need: 250 g of plain (all-purpose) flour plus extra for dusting; 1/2 teaspoon of salt; 50 g unsalted butter; 187 ml of milk; two bowls; access to a stove or microwave; tea towels; rolling pin; a non-stick pan. This recipe makes around six flatbreads and works well with wholewheat flour. Gluten-free options: it works pretty well with gluten-free flour but not almond flour. Vegan option: you can substitute the butter with olive oil and milk with almond milk.

Melt the butter in the milk on a stove or in a microwave. Combine the liquid with the flour and salt in a bowl. Use some of the extra flour to dust a work surface, and knead the mixture until the dough is smooth, around two minutes. Add extra flour if the dough is too sticky. Put the dough in a flour-dusted bowel, cover with a tea towel and let the dough rest for up to 30 minutes.

Cut the dough into six pieces, and roll each one into a ball. Dust the work surface with some more flour, then roll out each dough ball into 20 cm rounds, 2–3 mm thick.

Get an adult to heat a non-stick pan (with no oil) over a high heat. (You can also do this over a campfire, if you are meeting outside.) Place one flatbread in the pan, cooking for 60–90 seconds. It should puff up dramatically. Once one side is golden, flip it and cook the other side for 45 seconds until it has golden spots and puffs up again. Stack the cooked breads and keep them wrapped with a tea towel – the moisture helps soften the surface.

Talk about how Jesus sent Peter and John to make preparations to eat the Passover. This is a meal Jewish people celebrate every year to remember that God delivered them from slavery in Egypt, during which they eat flatbread. Jesus took bread, gave thanks and broke it, and gave it to his disciples saying, 'This is my body given for you; do this in remembrance of me.'

I wonder... have you ever taken bread or wine in a Communion celebration?

9. Helping hand art (community art project)

You will need: large canvas/paper/bulletin board to display the project; large sheets of paper; pencils; pens/markers/crayons; scissors; glue/tape/stapler to stick the hands to the board

Write the words 'How can you give a helping hand?' on the board/canvas. Trace your arm/hand (or have a friend help you) on to the paper. Decorate or colour it. Brainstorm

some ways that you can help others and write them on the arm/hand you created. Once finished, add it to the communal art project.

Talk about some ways that God has equipped you to help others. Are you great at drawing or writing? Do you make people laugh when you tell jokes? Just like the arm you crafted, which is different from everyone else's, you have different skills and abilities.

I wonder… how can you bring God's kingdom by serving others with your unique skills and abilities?

10. Peace planes

You will need: paper; pencils or pens (you could also have examples of different ways to fold paper aeroplanes)

Have participants write a note of peace or encouragement. Fold the paper into a paper aeroplane. Feel free to test out the planes now but save them for Celebration time.

Talk about how, during Jesus' last meal with his friends, he told them that he leaves them with his peace – a peace only Jesus can give. John 14:27 says: 'Peace I leave with you; my peace I give you. I do not give to you as the world gives. Do not let your hearts be troubled and do not be afraid' (NIV).

I wonder… how can we share the peace of Christ with others? What words might help spread peace? What actions? Save your aeroplane for the Celebration, where we'll launch them as we share the peace of Christ with everyone.

Celebration

To begin the Celebration, the core scripture (Luke 22:7–28 and John 13) will be introduced in a narrator-driven, no-prep-needed skit. Actors can be selected prior to the beginning of the celebration or, alternatively, volunteers can be called for right before starting the Celebration. Numbers of actors (disciples) can be modified (increased/decreased) as needed to allow for all who wish to participate. Once the skit begins, the narrator will drive the action by introducing characters and instructing them what to do and how to act. Actions to be highlighted are italicised. There are no props required for this skit – actors are encouraged to pretend to use any items discussed (e.g. when Jesus takes off his coat, he can simply mime taking a coat off.)

Skit cast: Jesus, Simon Peter, John, disciples (as many or as few as needed)

Skit setting/directions: the action should begin to the right or left of the centre of the room. Peter and John will lead the disciples to the centre of the room (upper room) for the main action of the skit.

Picture this… It was just before the Passover Festival, a time of feasting and celebration as the Jewish people remembered God delivering their people out of Egypt.

Jesus and his disciples are walking in Jerusalem. They are getting hungry after all the walking. See how *they rub their bellies looking sad. Jesus stops walking and halts the disciples by holding his hands out. He points at Peter and John.* He is telling them to go and find a place for their Passover feast.

Peter and John lead the disciples to the upper room where they'll celebrate the Passover; *Jesus hangs behind.* Peter and John are happy that they were able to follow Jesus' directions and find the upper room. *They give each other high-fives.*

The disciples are now gathered together for the feast. See how *they laugh and slap each other on the back in celebration.*

Look! *Jesus is entering the room.* Even though Passover was a time of celebration, Jesus looks sad. See how *Jesus frowns.* Jesus knows that the time will soon be here for him to leave this world.

Before he must go, however, Jesus has some things he needs to do, some lessons he needs to teach.

The disciples have finished eating. *They now rub their bellies with smiles on their faces.* It was delicious!

Watch as *Jesus draws the disciples' attention by raising his arms and waving them around. All the disciples are looking at Jesus now. Jesus picks up a piece of bread. He raises and holds the bread above his head and then breaks it in two.* Jesus is now telling them, 'This is my body broken for you. When you do this, remember me.' *Jesus sets the bread down and raises a cup with both hands above his head.* He is telling the disciples, 'This cup is the new covenant by my blood, which is poured out for you.'

The disciples look confused. See how *they shake their heads and shrug their shoulders.* They don't yet understand why Jesus is saying the things he is saying.

Jesus has one more lesson for the disciples. Watch as *Jesus takes off his coat, rolls up his sleeves, and grabs a towel, which he ties around his waist.* The disciples don't know what Jesus is doing. They look confused. *The disciples turn to each other and shrug* – no one knows what Jesus is doing.

Jesus pours water into a large bowl and begins to wash his disciples feet.'

The disciples look even more confused. What is going on?

Jesus is getting ready to wash Simon Peter's feet now. See how *he re-rolls up his sleeves and re-ties the towel at his waist.* Simon Peter tells Jesus 'No!' See how *he steps back from Jesus and covers his feet with his hands.*

Jesus knows that Simon Peter is confused. *He puts his arm around him and whispers to Simon Peter* that he must let him wash his feet if he wants to be his follower.

Simon Peter agrees. See how *he nods his head and points to his hands and head.* He's telling Jesus, 'Not just my feet but my hands and my head as well!'

Jesus continues to wash his disciples' feet, every single one. When he is finished, *he unties the towel around his waist and puts his coat back on.*

Jesus stands before the group and explains the lesson he just gave them. Watch how *Jesus raises his arms and gestures* as he tells the disciples that they should do what he did for them: serve.

Jesus tells his disciples that he has just a little time left. See how *he taps on his watch.* Jesus gives the disciples one last very important command. Jesus *holds up one finger and shakes it* and tells the disciples that they must love one another like he has loved them.

The disciples hear Jesus. *They make the heart symbol with their hands.*

I wonder...
- What the world would be like if everyone received the peace that Jesus offers?
- How the disciples felt when Jesus washed their feet?
- How can we show love and serve others like Jesus did?

Prayer
Have everyone bring their peace planes with them. Form a giant circle and then give the signal for everyone to launch their planes into the centre.

Lord, we receive your peace.
All: Help us to spread peace to others.
Lord, we receive your teaching.
All: Help us to share your teaching with others.
Lord, we receive your love.
All: Help us to love others in your name. Amen!

This is a good opportunity to share Communion with your Messy Church, using the flatbread from activity 8. Remember to speak in advance with your local ordained minister. You might want to use this guide developed for Messy Churches in Anglican settings – **messychurch.brf.org.uk/latest/resources/holy-communion-in-messy-church**.

Song suggestions
'I've got peace like a river' – Mission Praise #353
'The perfect example' (with hand motions) – Seeds Kids Worship
'The "do" song' – Paul McIntyre

Meal suggestions
Chicken nuggets with an assortment of dips or sauces along with chips or crisps and salad. If cooking outside, you might like to make pizza pitta bread pockets. Slice open a pitta bread, put in your favourite pizza topping, wrap in foil and cook over a grill on the firepit.

Session material: May
Is God real? Remember me!
by Jocelyn and Alex Czerwonka

 PDF DOWNLOAD  MESSY CHURCH AT HOME  MESSY CHURCH GOES WILD

Bible story for prep

Luke 24 (NRSV)

On that same day two of them [followers of Jesus] were going to a village called Emmaus… While they were talking and discussing, Jesus himself came near and went with them, but their eyes were kept from recognising him… When he was at the table with them, he took bread, blessed and broke it, and gave it to them. Then their eyes were opened, and they recognised him…

While they [the discples] were talking about this, Jesus himself stood among them and said to them, 'Peace be with you.' They were startled and terrified… He said to them, 'Why are you frightened…? Look at my hands and feet…' He showed them his hands and his feet… and he said to them, 'Have you anything here to eat?' They gave him a piece of broiled fish, and he took it and ate in their presence.

Luke 24:13–43 (abridged)

Pointers

Is God real? The question assumes that God can be placed into a category of 'things' alongside other things. Christians believe God is beyond all categories of 'things' known through our senses, for God is the creator of all such lesser things. Trying to fit God within creation is like saying an author is just a character within one of their books. A fictional character can reveal something of the author's mind and personality but not all of it. The fullness of God may not be revealed in our limited experience of reality, but we can still discover something of God in our world and life. We can learn about God through creation. The galaxies, stars and planets reveal God's power and beauty. The wonders of life reveal God's provision and purpose. Human history reveals God's plan for humanity, both as a whole and for every person. Scientific discoveries reveal God's amazing intelligence, and we recognise some of that intelligence in ourselves. With God's presence in our own hearts, we learn kindness, respect and consideration for others. There is so much to explore about the reality of God in this amazing world. And God has left clues, signs and treasures that we can start exploring today. However much we discover, there will always be more because God's reality is beyond our full knowledge.

Christians believe that enough of God is revealed in Jesus Christ to enable a living relationship with God. Through this relationship we share in some of God's qualities, such as compassion, love, forgiveness and much more. When Jesus was on earth he taught us much about God. So, when Jesus was put to death on the cross, his disciples were deeply shocked. In panic, the women and the men searched desperately for him. The authorities hastily arranged a cover up. There was a violent earthquake! Where could he be? What had happened? Then mysterious angels left messages. Women going to preparing Jesus' body for burial could not find it; instead, while hurrying though the garden graveyard they encountered him alive! In John 20:15 Mary Magdalene mistakes him for a gardener. Two sad disciples on the way to Emmaus unknowingly encountered Jesus along the road. When his identity was revealed during a meal at a roadside inn, they rushed back to the disciples, and found Jesus there. To convince them further, Jesus asked for food and ate it and showed them his wounded hands.

- Sometimes we feel that God is missing.
- We can encounter God in surprising places and ways.
- Jesus likes to meet us as we journey, offer hospitality, share a meal and gather for worship.
- Interruptions when we are rushing are sometimes opportunities for meeting Jesus.
- Shocking events and changes can disturb our trust in God.
- Mistaken expectations and even deliberate deception can sometimes prevent us from seeing the reality of God.

How does this session help people grow in Christ?

This session encourages us to be more observant of everything happening, not only being absorbed by what affects us, just as Jesus wants us to look upwards and outwards to him and to the world. It helps us to realise that there is more to Jesus than first impressions may reveal. We can learn that even in disaster and loss we can grow strong by trusting God's plan. It also shows us that by noticing clues, signs and treasures in the Bible and in this amazing world, we can discover the reality of Jesus.

Add value

Mealtime card

- What would it be like if Jesus sat and ate with you?
- Jesus called Mary by name and then she recognised him. What are the names of the people sitting near you at the table today?
- Have you ever taught someone? Who did you teach? What did you teach them?

Question to start and end the session

So… is God really real?

Social action idea

When Jesus appeared to the disciples, he asked them for something to eat. They gave him a piece of cooked fish. Fish is a good source of protein. Bring tins of fish to Messy Church to donate to a local food bank.

Activities

1. Empty tomb prayer space

You will need: items to create an empty tomb, e.g. a small tent or large cardboard boxes or a table with sheets draped over; a white sheet; a roll-mat to lie on; copies of Luke 24:1–12

Recreate the empty tomb. You could cut a large cardboard circle for the stone that's been rolled away. Place the folded sheet inside to represent grave clothes and a roll-mat for people to lie on.

Talk about what people read in Luke 24:1–12. Invite them to take turns to lie down in the tomb and spend time in quiet prayer. They could ask God questions. Remember to pause and notice what thoughts pop into your head. This is one way God might speak to you today.

I wonder… what questions do you have about this story? What questions do you have about God? Is God real?

2. Be a bubble photographer

You will need: cameras – invite people to bring cameras and have a few spares for those who don't have them; bubble mix and bubble wands; plants, flowers, mosses, lichen, bugs and butterflies to photograph

Start by making your own bubble wands using wire coat hangers, lengths of garden twist ties and/or pipe cleaners twisted around twigs. Cover any sharp ends with tape.

An outdoor area is ideal for this activity; alternatively have a nature table or nature wall and potted plants. Working in pairs, find a suitable photo subject; one person blows the bubbles and the other photograps the bubble. Take a photo of the subject first and then through a bubble to compare.

Optional extra: Photo competition. Email their best bubble photos to a Messy Church leader for judging.

Talk about what you notice about the bubbles? Are bubbles real? Can you catch them? Do the bubbles make the object clearer or more distinctive? Did you capture any reflections in the bubble photograph? Did the photo turn out the way you wanted it to be?

I wonder… what do you think bubbles teach us about God? Could we look through a bubble and see a glimpse of God?

Download support material at **messychurch.org.uk/getmessyvol2-2878**

3. Rosemary oil

You will need: branches of rosemary; olive oil; small glass jars or bottles with lids; 'Remember me' labels; string; scissors; a funnel

Use fresh rosemary. Crush a little rosemary in your hands and smell it. Cut sprigs of rosemary and add them to clean, dry bottles. Fill the bottles with olive oil, seal them with a lid, and then decorate them, attaching the labels with string.

Interesting myth: there is a myth that rosemary had white flowers, but when the virgin Mary was resting on her journey to Egypt, she spread her blue cloak over a white blossomed rosemary bush and the flowers turned from white to blue!

Talk about how rosemary is known as a memory herb or herb for remembrance. The women who went to the tomb of Jesus carrying spices 'remembered' his words: 'The Son of Man must be handed over to… sinners and be crucified and on the third day rise again' (Luke 24:7, NRSV).

I wonder… what other clues and words did Jesus tell us to 'remember him'?

4. Create a mural storyline

You will need: 3–4 metres in length of butchers paper or newsprint spread over two or three tables; pencils; crayons; paints; paper; scissors; glue; Bibles or printouts of Luke 24:1–49

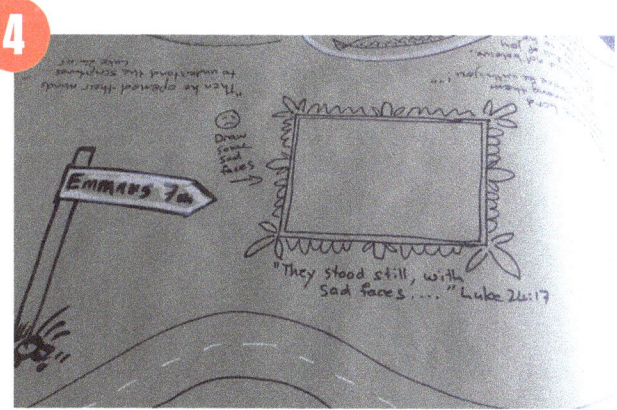

The aim of this activity is to take people on a journey through encounters people had with Jesus from the tomb, to Emmaus and back to Jerusalem again. Ahead of time, draw outlines of scenes and write snippets of scripture from Luke 24:1–49. For example, begin with setting the scene by writing 'Very early on Sunday morning' and draw an outline of a sunrise to be coloured in or painted; draw an outline of flowers or trees for the garden by the tomb; draw bright shining clothes for the two men. Suggest that people fill in the gaps in your outline with drawings of their own or prayers. For example, they could trace around hands at the part of the story where Jesus says, 'Look at my hands.'

Talk about the many people who encountered Jesus after his resurrection.

I wonder… how do we encounter Jesus today? What can we do to 'remember' Jesus?

Photocopying not permitted except under the CLA Church Licence.

5. Look at my hands!

You will need: different coloured paints; paint trays; brushes; water for cleaning brushes; crayons or felt-tips; a bowl of water and towels for washing hands

Create fish paintings by first drawing an eye and mouth where the painted heel of your hand will be. Then cover paint trays with different colours of paint. Coat your hand well with paint, and place it on the paper with the heel over the mouth and eye. You can combine colours on your hand if you want to have a 'two-tone' fish. Name your fish and allow to dry. NB: If your activity is near the mural you may want to add handprints to that as well.

Talk about how the disciples were terrified when Jesus appeared and thought they had seen a ghost! He said, 'Look at my hands.' He was also hungry, and they gave him a piece of cooked fish to eat (Luke 24:37–43). It might feel squishy and yuk placing your hands in paint, but as you do, think about how the disciples felt. Imagine their surprise when Jesus ate the fish!

I wonder… how do you think the disciples felt when Jesus appeared with them? How would you have reacted?

6. Nailed!

You will need: plywood or timber offcuts about A4-size; nails and hammers; fish template; coloured wool; scissors; felt-tips

Using the fish template, hammer the nails into the board as an outline. Tie a thread of wool to a nail and weave it around the outline, twisting it around the different nails as you go. Then weave the thread back and forth across the outline to create a pattern. Using different colours will add to the effect.

Talk about what fishy stories you can remember, either from the gospels or your own experiences.

I wonder… why did the resurrected Jesus eat some fish in front of his disciples?

7. Game – in the water/ on the road

You will need: a large space; chalk or masking tape to mark out areas

Divide a large space into three areas using the chalk or tape or existing lines made by floorboards, etc. The central area is called 'the road' and the outer areas called 'the water'. Participants are gathered into the central area as the rules are explained.

Rules: when the caller says, 'in the water', participants jump into the water. When the caller says, 'on the road', everyone jumps on to the road. The last person to jump and get to the right area is out of the game. The last person to be caught out becomes the next caller.

A leader is chosen as the caller, who gets the game started with this narrative:

When Jesus was born his family escaped Herod's soldiers by going to Egypt – on the road!

Jesus found his first disciples by Lake Galilee – in the water!

Jesus travelled all around Israel teaching and healing people – on the road!

Jesus made breakfast on the beach when his disciples went fishing – in the water!

Jesus met two disciples travelling to Emmaus – on the road!

Then speed and mix things up gradually:
in the water/on the road/in the water/on the road, etc.

This is a fast-paced game and can burn a lot of energy in a short time, but it can get boring if it goes on too long.

Talk about how those on the road with Jesus in those early days were regarded as being a disciple. Early Christians were called followers of 'the Way' (Acts 24:14).

I wonder… who are you following?

8. Plant forget-me-not seeds

You will need: seed raising mix and containers; seeds; wooden spoons; water in spray bottle

Sow seeds, lightly water them and take them home to grow. While the common forget-me-not plant is far from endangered, the Chatham Island forget-me-not (*Myosotidium hortensia*) is listed as 'nationally vulnerable' (**doc.govt.nz/nature/native-plants/chatham-island-forget-me-not**). Alternatively, choose seeds from an endangered plant species to grow.

Talk about sharing Gods love with others is a way we can spread seeds of his love and ensure he is always remembered.

I wonder… how do you remember Jesus? Who could you share some of God's love with today?

9. Remember me

You will need: a tray filled with 'remember me' objects, such as rosemary twig, spices, cross, nails, white cloth, angel decoration, sone, bread on plate, cup or goblet, Bible, fish; a cloth to cover; pens; paper

Take ten seconds to look at the tray and remember as many objects as possible. Cover the tray. Write down or draw all the objects you remember seeing.

Talk about how the word 'remember' was used often by Jesus as a clue that we would need reminders to 'remember him by'. What helped you to remember what was on the tray? You can use the objects on the tray to retell today's Bible story in Luke 24.

I wonder… how do we know if God is real?

10. Cooking for an unexpected guest

You will need: a pikelet recipe; pikelet mixture; electric frying pans; a whisk; a spoon; oil/butter; fish slices (pancake turner); clean tea towels; plates and spoons; jam and whipped cream to serve (optional)

Warning: Adult supervision will be required to avoid burns on hot fry pans. Ensure electric cords are safely secured and not a tripping or tipping hazard.

Prepare the pikelet mixture according to recipe. Do not overmix. As you cook pikelets, watch the bubbles form, then disappear, indicating it's now time to turn them over to cook on the other side.

Talk about the surprise when the two followers of Jesus invited him to stay overnight and eat with them after their long walk to Emmaus. Jesus took bread, said a blessing, broke the bread and gave it to them. Then their eyes were opened and he disappeared from their sight!

I wonder… what would it have been like to see Jesus again, but just as your eyes are opened, he disappears?

Celebration

Invite everyone to gather into a circle and to sit down. Those who have been at the different tables are invited to share one thing they liked about their activity or game. Try to name each activity for responses so be prepared by knowing what each activity was called. Point out that the session is based on a question: 'Is God real?' Check to see if their sessions helped them find an answer. You could ask: 'What is it about (nature, bubbles, a special memory, a good walk, people, Jesus, etc.) that makes you believe God is real?'

We are going to celebrate what we have done together first by having a big conversation in which the leaders say something and if you want to, you can reply in a big loud voice. After this we will have a conversation with God using bubbles. Firstly, let's stand up and get noisy.

Cue everyone that after the leader speaks, they call out 'Yes! God is real!'

Leader 1: When the stars were young, and the world was new, and people appeared on earth, they wondered: is God real? And the earth, and the sun, and the stars in heaven all cried out:
All: Yes! God is real!
Leader 2: When Jesus walked on earth to heal, teach and save, the people wondered: is God real? And the sparrows, and lilies and even stones cried out:
All: Yes! God is real!
Leader 3: After the cross and empty tomb, Jesus seemed to have gone; fearfully hiding, the disciples wondered: is God real? And we, with them all cry out:
All: Yes! God is real!
Leader 4: As two disciples walked to Emmaus they wondered: is Jesus' resurrection real? Jesus joined them and explained it all! They rushed back to Jerusalem to tell the others and cried out:
All: Yes! God is real!
Leader 5: As the disciples were gathered, Jesus stood among them saying, 'Peace be with you'. They wondered: is Jesus real? He showed them the scars on his hands and feet and ate some fish. They cried out:
All: Yes! God is real!
Leader 6: Around the world, today and tomorrow, wherever people are sad, or hurt, or hungry, in their hearts they wonder: is God real? With reaching hands and giving hearts we answer them:
All: Yes! God is real!

Invite everyone now to sit down and be still for a moment, to reflect and pray.

I wonder...
- Is it easy or hard for you to believe that God is real?

Tell the person next to you, or quietly think in your head, about the things that get in the way of believing that God is real. Have a chat with God about your thoughts, doubts or questions.

Prayer
Take time to remember and pray about special concerns in your community. Finish with this interactive prayer. You will need: bubble solution and wands for all ages.

Leader: Is God real?
All: Yes. (*loud voices*)
Leader: Can you see him in the flowers?
All: Yes.
Leader: Can you see him in the bugs?
All: Yes.
Leader: Can you see him in the trees?
All: Yes.
Leader: Can you see him in the stars?
All: Yes.
Leader: Can we know him in our hearts?
All: Yes.
Leader: Shall we bubble Gods love all over the world?
All: Yes (*Everyone blows bubbles as a thank you to God!*)
All: AMEN!

Song suggestions
'Is God real?' – Kasey Chambers
'God is real' – The Sound
'God's not dead, no! He is alive' – public domain
'This is amazing grace' – Phil Wickham
'This little light of mine' – public domain

Meal suggestions
Fish burgers (bread rolls served with boneless pieces of fish) are a good reminder of how, in his post-resurrection appearances, Jesus broke bread and ate a piece of fish in front of his disciples. As a drink, offer cold water with sprigs of rosemary. For dessert, have a chocolate fish with ice cream and/or rice bubble slice.

You could say the words of this grace before the meal:

We remember that when Jesus said a blessing and broke bread with the two travellers to Emmaus, their eyes were opened and they recognised Jesus. As we break bread together in this meal, may we welcome each other and Jesus among us. Amen.

Download support material at **messychurch.org.uk/getmessyvol2-2878**

Session material: June
Who is the Holy Spirit?
by Great Barr Messy Church

 PDF **DOWNLOAD**  MESSY CHURCH **AT HOME**  MESSY CHURCH **GOES WILD**

Bible story for prep

Acts 2:1–13 (NLT)

On the day of Pentecost all the believers were meeting together in one place. Suddenly, there was a sound from heaven like the roaring of a mighty windstorm, and it filled the house where they were sitting. Then, what looked like flames or tongues of fire appeared and settled on each of them. And everyone present was filled with the Holy Spirit and began speaking in other languages, as the Holy Spirit gave them this ability.

At that time there were devout Jews from every nation living in Jerusalem. When they heard the loud noise, everyone came running, and they were bewildered to hear their own languages being spoken by the believers.

They were completely amazed. 'How can this be?' they exclaimed. 'These people are all from Galilee, and yet we hear them speaking in our own native languages! Here we are – Parthians, Medes, Elamites, people from Mesopotamia, Judea, Cappadocia, Pontus, the province of Asia, Phrygia, Pamphylia, Egypt, and the areas of Libya around Cyrene, visitors from Rome (both Jews and converts to Judaism), Cretans, and Arabs. And we all hear these people speaking in our own languages about the wonderful things God has done!' They stood there amazed and perplexed. 'What can this mean?' they asked each other.

But others in the crowd ridiculed them, saying, 'They're just drunk, that's all!'

Pointers

This session draws from several different biblical references to help us learn together about how the Holy Spirit is present and at work in the world. We learn how the Holy Spirit was and is involved in creation. We explore how our bodies are a temple of the Holy Spirit (1 Corinthians 6:1). We learn how Jesus receives the Holy Spirit at baptism (Luke 3:2) and how that gift is for us too. Many of the activities, and particularly the celebration, use Acts 2, as we reflect together on the coming of the Holy Spirit on and into the lives of all Jesus' followers.

How does this session help people grow in Christ?

As we learn about how the Holy Spirit was at work in biblical times, we explore together how we can know the Holy Spirit is still at work. By sharing biblical stories and personal experience, we will learn from God and one another how the Spirit continues to touch our lives today.

Add value

Mealtime card
- What have you learnt about the Holy Spirit today?
- What is your favourite image of the Holy Spirit: water, wind, fire or a dove? Why?
- Does anyone want to share a story of how they have experienced the Holy Spirit?

Question to start and end the session
So… what do we know about the Holy Spirit and how can we tell the Holy Spirit is with us?

Social action idea
Why not go out in small groups or as a whole church and do a litter pick around your meeting place or home? (Some councils lend out litter pickers and high-visibility jackets.) If anyone asks why you are picking up litter, tell them about how the Holy Spirit gives us strength and courage to do things.

Additional copies can be purchased at **brfonline.org.uk/new-get-messy** or using the order form on page 72.

Activities

1. The Holy Spirit hovering over the waters

You will need: a play parachute

Start by playing some parachute games as a warm-up, e.g. lifting the parachute up and down, inviting people to run underneath and swap places if, for example, they have blonde hair, are wearing trainers, have a birthday in January, etc. When excess energy has been run off, lift up the parachute and have everyone sit on the edge of the parachute inside the dome created underneath. Share the 'Talk about' section and then hold silence. If you have anyone who has claustrophobia, you could begin with silence and then the conversation could be had on top of the parachute.

Talk about how the Holy Spirit was present at the beginning of creation, hovering over the waters. Talk about how the Holy Spirit is one of the ways we experience God's presence with us as comforter, helper and guide. If people are willing, invite both adults and children to share their experience and understanding of the Holy Spirit.

I wonder... have you experienced the Holy Spirit?

2. Giant marble run

You will need: lots of cardboard tubes (cut the ends of crisp tubes); masking tape; ping pong balls; a jug of water

Build a giant marble run (outside if possible). Test the 'run' with a few ping pong balls. When everyone has had a turn, and if you are brave enough, or have an outside space, take a jug of water and pour it through the tubes.

Talk about how the Bible describes our bodies as a temple of the Holy Spirit (1 Corinthians 6:19–20). Share how sometimes it can feel like the Holy Spirit is flowing through us, like the water (or the ping pong ball) running through the tubes, filling us and reaching parts of us we did not know needed God's presence.

I wonder... have you ever experienced this feeling?

3. S'mores

You will need: a BBQ or firepit, or tealights; wooden skewers; chocolate-coated biscuits; marshmallows (avoid gelatine in the ingredients if possible)

Put a marshmallow on a skewer and toast over a flame until it begins to melt, then place it between two biscuits, chocolate on the inside, and eat.

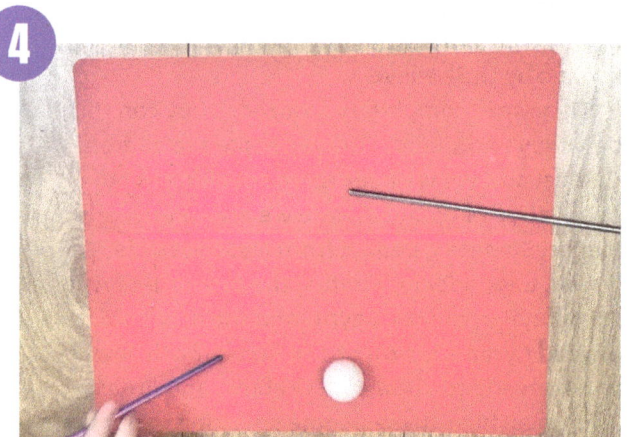

Talk about how the fire changes the marshmallow. The Holy Spirit is sometimes described as a burning fire that comes to change and transform us and help us to follow Jesus.

I wonder… are you scared or excited, or perhaps 'scited' (scared and excited), about the thought that the Holy Spirit can transform us?

4. Ping pong 'blowball'

You will need: oblong trays; ping pong balls; paper or metal straws

Two people each have a straw and stand/sit at either short side of the tray. Each player tries to score a goal by blowing the ping pong ball to the far side of the tray.

Talk about how Jesus' disciples felt the Holy Spirit like a rushing wind at Pentecost. Explain how sometimes the Holy Spirit takes us in different directions, and it can feel like we're being blown along at speed, while at other times it can feel like we're out of control.

I wonder… which direction will God take you in?

5. Free water play

You will need: a water table or bowls of water; bath toys or sieves; washed recycled plastic pots; bottles; containers

Encourage people of all ages to play with the water and containers. Invite them to watch, feel and listen to the water.

Talk about how John baptised his disciples and how Jesus came to John for baptism. Explain how the water of baptism is symbolic of a fresh start, a new beginning on a journey of faith. Ask if people were baptised as a child or as an adult. Invite them to think about making a fresh start or starting a new chapter in their faith journey, and if they would like, to splash or sprinkle water on themselves as a reminder of their baptism.

I wonder… are you looking for a fresh start?

6. Breath-powered rafts

You will need: a paddling pool; sticks gathered from outside; string; large leaves

Tie some sticks together with string to make the base of a raft. Attach a stick at right angles to form a mast. Make two slots in the leaf and thread it on to the mast. Place the raft in the pool and see what happens when you blow behind the leaf.

Talk about the transforming power of the Holy Spirit. Explain that just as the raft is propelled along the water by using our breath, if we allow God to work in our lives, the Holy Spirit will help us in our journey through life, changing and transforming us into the best version of ourselves we can be. You may notice that the boat stops when you stop blowing. We too can run out of breath on our journey with God if we don't take time to return to the source to be filled once more with the breath of life.

I wonder… how do you make space to be filled with God's Spirit? What does that look like for you?

7. Birthday cake

You will need: weighing scales; margarine; eggs; caster sugar; self-raising flour; flavouring; a cake tin; icing sugar; jam; candles; matches

Invite different members of the group to add the ingredients to make a simple sponge cake (you can find lots of simple recipes online). Make sure everyone has a chance to stir the cake. While the cake is baking, make some butter icing. Once the cake has cooled, invite others to sandwich the cake together, ice it and put candles on top.

Talk about how the Holy Spirit gives everyone different gifts so that we can work together to share God's love throughout the world. Explain that the coming of the Holy Spirit at Pentecost (Acts 2) is sometimes described as the birthday of the church. At the end of your meal, light the candles and sing 'Happy birthday' to your Messy Church and then share the cake.

I wonder… how do you like to celebrate a birthday?

8. Origami dove prayers

You will need: paper; simple instructions for making the dove (easily found online)

Create a prayer space with cushions, fabric drapes or a pop-up tent. Encourage this activity to be done quietly unless help is needed in following the instructions!

Talk about how when Jesus was baptised, the Holy Spirit came down upon him like a dove (Luke 3:2). The dove is often used as a sign of peace. In many situations, the Holy Spirit is needed to bring peace and resolution to conflict. As you fold your dove, pray for peace.

I wonder… what situations need the Holy Spirit to bring peace and an end to conflict?

9. Tongues of fire

You will need: sticks; clean transparent yoghurt pots/plastic cups; scraps of red, yellow and orange paper (or tissue paper if you have it); PVA glue; glue spreaders

Pour some PVA glue into the bottom of the yoghurt pot. Break up the sticks and put them into the pot to build a base for your fire. Then add scraps of the coloured paper to make the 'flames'.

Talk about how when the Holy Spirit appeared among the disciples at Pentecost, it looked like tongues of fire. Tell the story of how when Jesus met his friends on the Emmaus Road and began explaining things to them, it felt like their hearts were burning within them. Encourage people to take their 'fires' home with them and each time they see them, to invite God to help them understand more about the Holy Spirit.

I wonder... what questions do you have about the Holy Spirit burning inside of you?

10. The dove from above

You will need: a printed copy of Luke 3:22; a card dove template; spare recycled food packaging boxes; scraps of material; PVA glue; glue spreaders; string; a hole punch; scissors

Use the template to cut out your own dove shape. Make a hole at the top of the dove's body. Tie a length of string through the hole. Glue the material scraps on either side of the dove template. Take your dove home and tie it to a curtain rail.

Talk about the story in Luke 3:22. A dove descended on Jesus at his baptism. It was a sign of God's presence with him. When you see your dove hanging at home, remember that God is always with you too. Read the Bible verses again. Listen to God saying, 'You [name] are my dearly loved child, and you bring me great joy.'

I wonder... where or when do you notice God's presence with you?

Celebration

Begin the celebration by asking some questions:

Which was your favourite activity? Why?

Did you learn anything new about the Holy Spirit? What?

Does anyone want to share their experience of the Holy Spirit?

Has anyone got any questions about the Holy Spirit?

Tell the following story (script based on Acts 2) and encourage participation. You will need the tongues of fire from activity 9.

On the day of Pentecost all the believers were meeting together in one place. Suddenly, there was a sound from heaven like the roaring of a mighty windstorm *(encourage wind sounds),* and it filled the house where they were sitting *(encourage louder wind sounds).*

Then, what looked like flames or tongues of fire appeared and settled on each of them *(invite people to put their 'tongues of fire' on their heads).*

And everyone present was filled with the Holy Spirit and began speaking in other languages, as the Holy Spirit gave them this ability *(encourage people to speak in languages other than your local language, or gobbledygook if they don't know any other languages).*

At that time there were devout Jews from every nation living in Jerusalem. When they heard the loud noise, everyone came running, and they were bewildered to hear their own languages being spoken by the believers *(encourage people to speak more loudly in languages other than your local language, or gobbledygook if they don't know any other languages).*

They were completely amazed. 'How can this be?' they exclaimed *(get people to repeat, 'How can this be?').*

'These people are all from Galilee, and yet we hear them speaking in our own native languages! Here we are – Parthians, Medes, Elamites, people from Mesopotamia, Judea, Cappadocia, Pontus, the province of Asia, Phrygia, Pamphylia, Egypt and the areas of Libya around Cyrene, visitors from Rome (both Jews and converts to Judaism), Cretans and Arabs' *(if you have A/V facilities, show a map marking these places and point them out).*

'These people are all from Galilee, and yet we hear them speaking in our own native languages! And we all hear these people speaking in our own languages about the wonderful things God has done!'

They stood there amazed and perplexed. 'What can this mean?' they asked each other.

But others in the crowd ridiculed them, saying, 'They're just drunk, that's all!'

I wonder...
- What the Holy Spirit is doing as we gather as Messy Church?
- How can I know that the Holy Spirit is living in me?
- How will I experience the Holy Spirit in the days and weeks to come?

Prayer
In small groups and with appropriate supervision, light a candle or a tealight. Watch the flame. Think about how flames bring light and warmth. Thank God for the times when you sense God's presence with you through the Holy Spirit, when the way forward seems clear.

Blow the candle out. Pray for those times when God takes you by surprise and takes you in a direction you are not expecting, or when you have no sense of God's Spirit being with you.

Take the candle home and use it in your prayers over the coming days, as a reminder of God's presence and power in your life.

Song suggestions
'This little light of mine' – Public domain
'Shine from the inside out' – Spring Harvest
'Pentecost Song' – Jan Brind (to the tune of 'The grand old duke of York')

Meal suggestions
How about having a barbeque, or if the forecast is bad, hot dogs prepared indoors? If the place where you meet allows, you could cook on a bonfire or fire pit. You could try baking potatoes in the fire and serving with grated cheese. For a sweet treat, you could cook bananas and chocolate wrapped in foil. These provide further opportunity to talk about the transforming work of the fire of the Holy Spirit.

Additional copies can be purchased at brfonline.org.uk/new-get-messy or using the order form on page 72.

Session material: July
'Come, follow me'
by May Dappa and Martyn Payne

Bible story for prep

Matthew 4:18–22 (NIV)

As Jesus was walking beside the Sea of Galilee, he saw two brothers, Simon called Peter and his brother Andrew. They were casting a net into the lake, for they were fishermen. 'Come, follow me,' Jesus said, 'and I will send you out to fish for people.' At once they left their nets and followed him.

Going on from there, he saw two other brothers, James son of Zebedee and his brother John. They were in a boat with their father Zebedee, preparing their nets. Jesus called them, and immediately they left the boat and their father and followed him.

Luke 5:27–28 (NIV)

After this, Jesus went out and saw a tax collector by the name of Levi sitting at his tax booth. 'Follow me,' Jesus said to him, and Levi got up, left everything and followed him.

Pointers

When Jesus invited people to follow him, they were going about their business. Andrew and Peter were throwing their net into the lake; James and John were preparing for a fishing trip; and Matthew (Levi) was sat in his tax office. The call to 'follow me' came during everyday living. We don't know how much these men already knew about Jesus or what they had already heard him say, but what is clear is that they chose to follow him. They left their day job for a new calling.

Becoming a disciple isn't an occasional add-on to our normal lives, nor a hobby for our spare time; it is all or nothing. The two sets of brothers by the lake discovered a new sort of fishing that would lead them far from home and off on a huge adventure with God; and the one who kept accounts for the Romans would end up writing an account of the life of Jesus that is still being read by millions across the world. I wonder what wonderful story yet to be written is waiting for those in your Messy Church who may respond in this session to the invitation to leave everything and follow Jesus.

How does this session help people grow in Christ?

As Jesus told stories and performed many miracles, he also invited people to follow him. It was unusual for a rabbi in those days to choose his disciples; it was normally students who applied to sit at the feet of well-known teachers. But Jesus is God come looking for us, and whose great love longs to welcome everyone into God's family. To become a disciple is all about living life the Jesus way; to learn by watching what Jesus said and did; to learn in conversation, as they walked the roads of Galilee and spent time with him; to learn by imitation, as an amateur learns a new skill alongside a professional, who gently corrects mistakes and inspires us to try again.

At their best, our Messy Churches offer young and old alike, a model of how to follow Jesus. As the generations work together, they pass on what faith means in the everyday. Through stories, songs and prayers, everyone's discipleship is nurtured; in conversation around the activity table or over the meal, we discover and explore the best life God has planned for us.

Following Jesus comes at a cost (Luke 14:2), but the reward is matchless. May this Messy Church session not only offer the invitation to follow Jesus but help us all become more and more like him as his disciples.

Add value

Mealtime card

- What new skills have you learned in this session?
- What new skills do you think the disciples learned by following Jesus?
- What might change in our lives as we follow Jesus?

Photocopying not permitted except under the CLA Church Licence.

Download support material at **messychurch.org.uk/getmessyvol2-2878**

Question to start and end the session
So… what helps you become a follower of Jesus?

Social action idea
Do you have a care home in your area? Young and old have so many skills they could teach each other. For example, older people may appreciate help with technology, while younger people have often missed out on some crafting skills, such as crocheting, knitting or cross-stitching, which older people could teach them. Why not approach the activities coordinator of your local care home to talk about how family groups from your Messy Church may grow in their discipleship as they both teach and learn skills in a different context.

Activities

1. Letters scramble

You will need: assorted letters on tiles or cubes, such as Scrabble tiles or letters from Bananagrams; a large container as a shaker; an egg timer or the timer on a mobile phone; a clear surface; paper and pencil for scores

Gather people into teams of two. Ideally each team should have people from different generations matched together. Put the assortment of letters into the shaker. The activity leader asks the teams in turn to choose twelve letters to take out, and then, in 30 seconds, using the tiles chosen, the challenge is to create a word or words from the letters, using as many of the twelve as possible. Keep a record of which team uses most letters successfully.

Talk about how Jesus chose twelve disciples to become a connected team who would work together with him to share the good news of God's love. If possible, link some of the words created to the Bible story. Notice how it's hard to use all the letters. The Bible talks about how some people started to follow Jesus, but found it too hard, so they gave up. Matthew 22:14 reminds us, 'Many are invited, but few are chosen.' Ask someone who's been a Christian for a while about the big and little changes they have made in their daily lives when they chose to follow Jesus.

I wonder… what makes it hard to be a follower of Jesus?

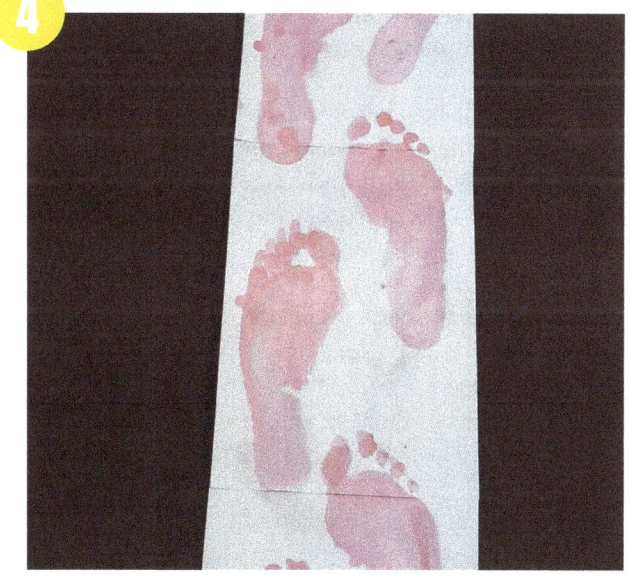

2. Learn a skill

You will need: an activity leader who is able to knit, crochet or cross-stitch, and who can bring the appropriate needles, hooks, wool or yarn

The leader should show the novice group how to get started with knitting/crocheting/cross-stitching. This

Photocopying not permitted except under the CLA Church Licence.

will be a learning-together experience which will require patience and perseverance, alongside attention to instructions.

Your first task is to make a slip knot: Take your yarn and leave a generous tail. Hold the yarn and bring the hands together to make a loop. Hold the loop that you have made in one hand. Grab the yarn that's unattached to the ball and bring it behind the loop. Pull the strand of yarn through the loop. This little loop is called a slipknot. You are ready to cast on with it!

Talk about how being a disciple of Jesus is like being an apprentice, learning by watching and copying from someone who already has a particular skill. The disciples learned how to care for strangers, pray to God and bring healing and help to others by watching Jesus and spending time with him. We can learn about Jesus when we read the Bible, but we can experience and put theory into practice when we are part of a Christ-centred community, journeying alongside more experienced Christians, guided by the Holy Spirit.

I wonder... who could you ask to encourage you and pray for you on your journey of following Jesus?

3. Trying something new

You will need: a couple of sandwich toasters; bread; butter; safe knives for cutting; a variety of toppings; kitchen roll; plates

Most people will be familiar with how to make a toasted sandwich, but there is of course a wide variety of possible fillings according to taste. Encourage adults and children to experiment with a variety of types of toasted sandwich using their favourite ingredients.

Talk about how the disciples put into practice what they had learned from Jesus, sometimes making mistakes but learning from them. A bit like the variety of possibilities for toasted sandwiches, disciples aren't clones of Jesus. Each follows the Lord in his or her own unique and gifted way.

I wonder... what are your unique gifts?

4. Messy footsteps

You will need: big sheets of plain lining paper to cover a wide area, ideally outdoors; a variety of footwear, including boots, wellingtons and sandals, in different sizes; some shallow trays, each with different coloured water-based paint inside; cloths and water available to clean hands, etc.; good supervision

An adult and a child should team up for this activity, putting on footwear, which is then dipped in the paint, or they could choose to dip their bare feet in pain instead. Holding hands, they should walk along the lining paper, creating a trail of footprints. As each pairing adds more footprints, they are creating a big picture of what discipleship looks like.

Talk about how Jesus invited people to follow him, both to walk alongside him and to walk in the way he did, just as he was walking in step with God. Jesus called the disciples to be followers who would bring others to follow in the footsteps of Christ.

I wonder... who could you invite to Messy Church?

5. Gone fishing

You will need: a cardboard box; printed images of fish and sea creatures for decorating inside and outside the box; a glue stick; a set of 15–20 fish images or fish shapes; adhesive magnetic strips; chopsticks; 2x magnets; string; sea-green cardboard/paper; scissors; decorative sticking tape

Make your own aquarium by cutting the sides of the cardboard box flaps off and stick the printed papers on four sides of the box, decorating it in and out. Line the edges with sticky tape. Create the bottom of the seabed by scrunching up the cardboard paper and sticking it on the bottom. Cut out a further 15–20 fish and stick some magnetic strips on one side. On twelve of the fish, write the names of the twelve disciples and mix them with the rest of the fish. Make some fishing rods by tying the string on to a chopstick, attaching the magnet at the end of the line. Put the string down in the box, to pick up a fish. The challenge is to fish out the twelve disciples.

Talk about how Jesus called the disciples to become 'fishers of people' – followers who would bring others into the kingdom of God.

I wonder... who could you invite to Messy Church?

6. Fruit kebabs

You will need: kebab sticks; twelve different types of fruit – e.g. grapes, watermelon chunks, strawberries, blackcurrants, orange slices, blueberries, pineapple chunks, banana slices, raspberries, mango chunks, peach slices, pear chunks; bowls with the fruit in; a place to wash hands before you start

Invite adults and children to arrange the fruit in a colourful pattern along the kebab stick as their chosen twelve fruit disciples.

Talk about how Jesus chose different sorts of people to be in his team, each with their own unique flavours of personality and personal tastes. As these are eaten, you might also like to introduce the idea of the fruits of the Spirit (as

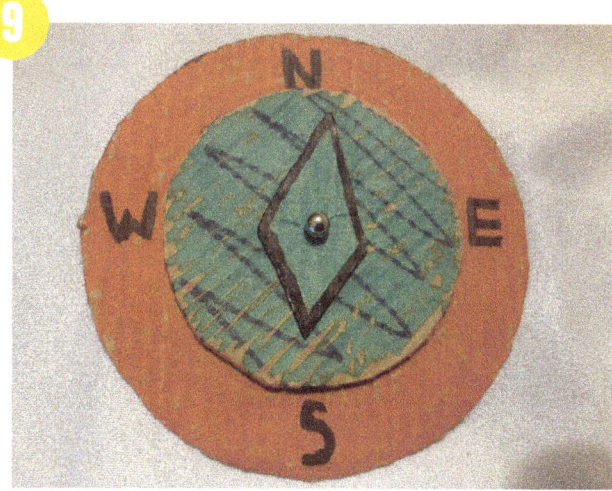

listed in Galatians 5:22–23) as some of the characteristics of disciples who follow Jesus.

I wonder… which fruit of the Holy Spirit (love, joy, peace, patience, goodness, kindness, faithfulness, gentleness and self-control) do you need help with?

7. Letting go

You will need: a collection of up to ten different items which most people carry about with them because they are important in some way – e.g. a mobile phone, a wallet, a sports membership card, a beloved toy, a book, a family photograph, a set of keys, tissues, a compact, a comb and a piece of jewellery, a Bible

This is a group activity in which one person has to make decisions about what they will let go of, advised and encouraged by the comments of others. The person choosing should pick up all the items and then be told that they can only take nine. Which one goes? But then they can only take seven. Which two others should go? And so on until only one item is left. Encourage debate!

Talk about how Jesus asked his followers to let go of their old lives to follow him instead. How easy or difficult was that, do you think? What might we need to let go of? People have always been tested to see if they will put the things of God first in their lives. Find someone at Messy Church who has given something up to follow Jesus – what did they let go of?

I wonder… what is God asking you to let go of?

8. Follow me

You will need: an outside area where an obstacle course has been set up. Include items to climb over or go under, both natural and human-made, such as trees, bushes, ladders or tables; an activity leader, who will show the way to go around the obstacle course, not just negotiating the hurdles, but also sometimes walking backwards or hopping, or skipping, etc. This should be an energetic outdoor activity.

The leader should gather his disciples, and in a line, they should follow the leader around the course, imitating him or her in every possible way.

Talk about how disciples are called to follow Jesus, being like him and representing him among family, friends and neighbours, in all they do and say.

I wonder… what did you find easy or difficult with this activity? What would help next time?

9. Make a disciple compass

You will need: A4 cardboard paper in two different colours; a glue stick; corrugated cardboard; felt-tip pen; a metal split paper fastener pin for the middle; a drawing compass (to make circles); scissors

Using the drawing compass, draw and then cut out two circles, one bigger than the other. Glue them together with the smaller paper in the middle. Cut the corrugated cardboard paper in a long diamond shape to represent the hand of the compass. Make a hole with a drawing compass and insert the metal split paper fastener pin. Draw N, S, E, W on the four sides of the larger circle and design the middle to your preference.

Talk about how Jesus is our magnetic north. He shows us the way to go and points us in the right direction. Disciples use the compass of Jesus as their navigation aid through life, reading about his way in the Bible, learning as apprentices in a Christ-centred community and, through praying, inviting the Holy Spirit to be a guide.

I wonder... who can encourage you on your discipleship journey?

10. Go on a disciple hunt

You will need: sets of twelve coins, made up from two each of 1p, 2p, 5p, 10p, 20p and 50p pieces; these need to be hidden around your Messy Church service area. Alternatively, you could use Lego pieces or marbles.

Children and adult teams are invited to search for a set of twelve-coin disciples, as they go on a hunt around Messy Church. This game could be used as a starter activity for the session.

Talk about how some of the disciples did come in pairs as brothers or friends, and in one case, Matthew knew all about coins as well.

I wonder... have you ever had to pick a winning team? If you were Jesus, who would you pick to be in your team?

Celebration

Jesus chooses the twelve disciples

What a load of difference we have here at Messy Church! Different names, different hairstyles, different skin colours, different shoe sizes, different heights, different widths(!), different voices, different talents, different characters, different personalities.

Invite everyone to pair up and then to spot some of the many differences between each other (the obvious and the unusual!)

What a load of difference we are! It's too much... too many... too scary! Most of us tend to prefer it when people are more like ourselves, when people have names we know, are more our size and share our ideas. But in today's Bible story we learn that God loves difference; in fact God made us to be different and it is through people who are different working together that God can show us more of what God is like. This is why Jesus chose a bunch of different disciples to follow him.

Jesus was faced by a load of differences. Some of his followers were young and some were old; some were clever and some were 'not so clever'; some were easily confused and some were very strong-minded; some were talented and some could only do one thing; some were angry and some were peaceful; some were suspicious and some were over-enthusiastic.

But Jesus knew he needed them all in his world-changing team.

And each time Jesus chose someone to follow him, the rest said: **We don't need you.** But Jesus said: **Oh yes we do!**

Rehearse this, to be called out at the appropriate points in the story! Twelve disciples are now going to be called. For each one, invite out someone from the Messy congregation, one at a time, to be that disciple, a mixture of adults and children, young and old, male and female.

Jesus chose hot-headed, loud-mouthed, never-stop-to-think-about-it **Peter**.

The rest said: **We don't need you.**

But Jesus said: **Oh yes we do!**

Jesus chose angel-faced, quick-to-smile, far-too-young-looking **John**.

The rest said: **We don't need you.**

But Jesus said: **Oh yes we do!**

Jesus chose quick-eyed, clever-in-class, good-at-languages **Andrew**.

The rest said: **We don't need you.**

But Jesus said: **Oh yes we do!**

Jesus chose grumpy-looking, stick-in-the-mud, 'I don't believe it!' **Nathaniel**.

The rest said: **We don't need you**.

But Jesus said: **Oh yes we do!**

Jesus chose very-excitable, won't-ever-give-up, always-in-a-rush **Philip**.

The rest said: **We don't need you!**

But Jesus said: **Oh yes we do!**

Jesus chose thoroughly nice, his-mummy-loves-him, he'll-go-far **James**.

The rest said: **We don't need you.**

But Jesus said: **Oh yes we do!**

Jesus chose good-with-money, rather-greedy, 'I'll do anything to succeed' **Matthew**.

The rest said: **We don't need you.**

But Jesus said: **Oh yes we do!**

Jesus chose never-trusting, always-doubting, 'I'm-not-sure-about-this' **Thomas**.

The rest said: **We don't need you.**

But Jesus said: **Oh yes we do!**

Jesus chose not-very-strong, easily overlooked, 'I'm-too-small' **James**.

The rest said: **We don't need you.**

But Jesus said: **Oh yes we do!**

Jesus chose temper-losing, tantrum-throwing, 'always ready-for-a-fight' **Simon**.

The rest said: **We don't need you.**

But Jesus said: **Oh yes we do!**

Jesus chose very-impatient, over-ambitious, 'I'll-do-it-my-way' **Judas**.

The rest said: **We don't need you.**

But Jesus said: **Oh yes we do!**

And finally, Jesus chose nobody-special, easily overlooked, 'what's his name?' **Jude**.

The rest said: **We don't need you.**

But Jesus said: **Oh yes we do!**

Yes, Jesus chose each one of these twelve disciples, with all their differences. And they became a great team. They became great friends working together. They learned togetherness as disciples of Jesus. They became a team that changed the world (with just one substitute before extra time!), because God can bring our differences together, to help each one of us become the best we can be. Jesus is calling you to be a disciple too.

I wonder...
- Will you follow Jesus?
- What are you willing to let go of to follow Jesus?
- What will be hardest to give up, to follow Christ?

Invite everyone to join in a discipleship conga and, following a leader, sing, to the conga rhythm, the following words:

Come, come, come, Jesus is our leader.
Come, come, come, we will follow him.
Come , come, come, anywhere he leads us.
Come, come, come, we will follow him.

Prayer
Use as a visual aid something from the messy footsteps activity, as you invite everyone to 'pray with their feet' while they echo the following prayer as they walk on the spot:

Lord Jesus, you call us, (**Lord Jesus, you call us,**)
to walk in your steps. (**to walk in your steps.**)
Help us to follow (**Help us to follow**)
the way that you go (**the way that you go**)
and be you disciples, (**and be you disciples,**)
with God's love on show. (**with God's love on show.**)
Amen and amen (**Amen and amen**)

Song suggestions
'Follow, follow, I will follow Jesus' (chorus from the hymn 'Down in the valley with my saviour I would go') – William Cushing
'I have decided to follow Jesus' – Mission Praise #272
'All to Jesus I surrender' – Mission Praise #25
'We're following Jesus' – Rob Evans

Meal suggestions
Toasted sandwiches and fruit kebabs from the activities. Pitta bread pizza. Pasta and tomato sauce.

Additional copies can be purchased at **brfonline.org.uk/new-get-messy** or using the order form on page 72.

Session material: August
Can I trust God? A new direction
by Sandy Brodine and Greg Ross

 **PDF** DOWNLOAD    **MESSY CHURCH** AT HOME    **MESSY CHURCH** GOES WILD

Bible story for prep

Acts 8:12; 26–40 (NRSV)

But when they believed Philip, who was proclaiming the good news about the kingdom of God and the name of Jesus Christ, they were baptised, both men and women...

Then an angel of the Lord said to Philip, 'Get up and go towards the south to the road that goes down from Jerusalem to Gaza.' (This is a wilderness road.) So he got up and went. Now there was an Ethiopian eunuch, a court official of the Candace, the queen of the Ethiopians, in charge of her entire treasury. He had come to Jerusalem to worship and was returning home; seated in his chariot, he was reading the prophet Isaiah. Then the Spirit said to Philip, 'Go over to this chariot and join it.' So Philip ran up to it and heard him reading the prophet Isaiah. He asked, 'Do you understand what you are reading?' He replied, 'How can I, unless someone guides me?' And he invited Philip to get in and sit beside him. Now the passage of the scripture that he was reading was this:

'Like a sheep he was led to the slaughter,
and like a lamb silent before its shearer,
so he does not open his mouth.
In his humiliation justice was denied him.
Who can describe his generation?
For his life is taken away from the earth.'

The eunuch asked Philip, 'About whom, may I ask you, does the prophet say this, about himself or about someone else?' Then Philip began to speak, and starting with this scripture he proclaimed to him the good news about Jesus. As they were going along the road, they came to some water, and the eunuch said, 'Look, here is water! What is to prevent me from being baptised?' He commanded the chariot to stop, and both of them, Philip and the eunuch, went down into the water, and Philip baptised him. When they came up out of the water, the Spirit of the Lord snatched Philip away; the eunuch saw him no more and went on his way rejoicing. But Philip found himself at Azotus, and as he was passing through the region he proclaimed the good news to all the towns until he came to Caesarea.

Pointers

Different parts of the Christian church practise baptism in different ways. Some traditions only baptise babies and children; others bless or dedicate babies and children and only baptise teenagers or adults. Some churches do both.

Whatever the practice of your tradition, Messy Church is generally not the place to promote one tradition or practice as better or more 'right' than another.

The most important thing about baptism is the mystery of what God does for us in baptism.

Make sure your 'leader', 'pastor', 'priest' or 'minister' is aware that you are having this theme and is present and has resourced your team.

Encourage people who are interested in being baptised or are curious to have various ways of following up with your church or their own tradition. It might be that Messy Church is the best place for the baptism to take place, but make sure you involve an ordained minister early on in the conversation. Here's some useful liturgy for an Anglican setting – **southwark.anglican.org/wp-content/uploads/2020/12/Messy-Celebration-baptism-liturgy.pdf**. You might also like to use the download resource 'Messy Basics' as part of your baptism preparation.

How does this session help people grow in Christ?

This session explores baptism: a sign of following Jesus and of being welcomed into and belonging to God's family. It provides an opportunity for those who have been baptised to 'remember' their baptism, and for those who have not to wonder if it is a gift they would like to receive.

Add value

Mealtime card
- Share a story of seeing someone be baptised or being baptised (if not yourself, perhaps a family member or friend).
- Do you know anything about Ethiopia? What continent is it in? What countries are its neighbours?
- How fast can you run? Would you be able to run as fast as Philip beside the chariot carrying the Ethiopian?

Question to start and end the session
So… what does being baptised mean for us today?

Social action idea
The Ethiopian in today's story found a pool of water beside the road, and he asked Philip to baptism him in it. Sadly in many countries, pools of water are too dangerous to even touch. The need for clean, safe, drinking water and toilets is a number one concern for millions of people around the world. In March 2023, a United Nations report estimated that around 2 billion people in the world do not have access to a safe water supply. This is roughly one in four people. Allocate everyone in your Messy Church celebration a number from one to four. Ask all the number ones to move to one side of the room and give them a glass of water that has been made brown with food colouring, while you give everyone else a clean glass of water. This is a visual representation of 25% of the world's population not having access to clean water.

Find out what agency of your church or community supports the development of clean drinking water, washing water and of safe toilets. See if you can raise some extra funds to support them. Toilet Twinning and Who Gives A Crap are just two organisations that fund clean water and toilet projects around the world.

Activities

1. Make a name bracelet

You will need: one toilet roll centre; four craft sticks; Sellotape; coloured paper; a wooden skewer; wool; letter beads. Alternatively, you could make name bracelets with pony beads, loom bands, handmade paper beads or in any other way you like.

Make your own 'spool knitting loom' by taking a toilet roll and taping four craft sticks to it. Decorate it by covering it in coloured paper. To make your knitted bracelet: drop the end of your yarn down the centre of your cardboard roll. Let a 10 cm tail hang out at the bottom. Keeping a gentle hold on the tail, cast on your stitches by wrapping your yarn around one craft stick once, in a clockwise direction, and then take your yarn to the second craft stick, winding it once in a clockwise direction. Move on to the third and fourth sticks in the same manner, wrapping the yarn around them once in a clockwise direction. To knit your stitches: lay your yarn across the first craft stick, just above the stitch that you cast on. With your fingers or the wooden skewer, hook the lower stitch over the top of the new stitch and let it fall into the centre of the tube. Gently pull the tail of the yarn to tighten the stitch. Continue around your loom, doing the same thing. Don't forget to keep giving the tail a gentle tug to tighten the stitches. When you are finished, attach some beads with your name to the bracelet.

Talk about when people are baptised, they often choose a new name with a special meaning; for example, Greg means watchful or vigilant. Sandy (from Cassandra) means shining upon or helping humankind.

I wonder… what does your name mean? Do you know why it was chosen for you? Is there anyone else in your family that has the same or a similar name?

2. Philip meets the Ethiopian official

You will need: Playdoh; large marshmallows; small skewers or cocktail sticks; round jellies; liquorice; jelly babies; icing

Make a horse from Playdoh. Attach two sticks to the large marshmallow and place the horse in between them, with a lace of liquorice as a 'harness' across the sticks. Attach the wheels to the chariot with other small pieces of stick. Use a tab of icing to secure the Ethiopian official in place.

Talk about how the Ethiopian was a follower of God, but may not have been welcomed into the temple in Jerusalem because he was not Jewish.

I wonder... have you ever felt excluded?

3. Ethiopian official

You will need: a disposable cup; a craft stick; a peg; chenille stems; some people figures (we made ours out of dolly pegs and felt – but you could use Lego figures, etc.)

Print some photos of Roman chariots from the internet and provide them for your community. Ask them to use the materials to creatively make a Roman chariot. The photo provided shows how one of our families completed this task. I wonder what your Messy families can do!

Talk about when Philip told the Ethiopian about God's love shown in Jesus, he was changed. He wanted to follow Jesus and to say that publicly before those travelling with him, so he asked Philip why he could not be baptised in the puddle of water.

I wonder... do you know of anyone who has been baptised in an unusual place? Get them to share their story.

4. Water play

You will need: a large ground sheet or waterproof picnic blanket turned upside down; water play utensils (see picture for ideas)

Use the water play utensils to make patterns on the ground sheet, or to have fun playing with the water. (Note: we did this indoors – but it's even better, and messier, if you're outdoors 'in the wild!')

Talk about how water supply is very different across the world. Some places have drought, so there's not enough water to grow food; other places have too much water, so land can get flooded and crops destroyed.

I wonder... what is your experience of water?

Download support material at **messychurch.org.uk/getmessyvol2-2878**

5. Holy Spirit peace prayers

You will need: a straw; the dove shape and paper rectangle cut out of the resource sheet; Sellotape; pens

Wrap the paper rectangle around the straw (not too tight) and then fold the top of the paper over to make a 'pocket' for the end of the straw. Make sure that there is a little gap between the fold of the pocket and the end of the straw or your paper will stick to the straw and will not fly. Write or draw prayers for people or places who need God's peace on the front of the dove shape. Turn the dove over and Sellotape the paper pocket to it. Turn the dove the right way round, aim it and then blow through the straw. Watch your peace dove fly as a symbol of giving the prayers to God! (You could also make this into a competition to see who can make their dove fly the furthest.)

Talk about the many parts of the world that need God's peace right now.

I wonder… what can you do to help bring about peace?

6. God's family quilt

You will need: fabric paints; squares of calico; sequins; glue; brushes; water pots

Give each family a square of calico and ask them to design a square for a big 'Messy Family Quilt' to celebrate the fact that all of the families in your Messy Church are a part of God's family! When you're finished, ask someone in your church community to sew all the squares together in a 'quilt' so it can be displayed in your church.

Talk about when we are baptised, we become part of God's family! But we all have our own families too.

I wonder… what is special about your family?

7. Wondering word prayers

You will need: letter tiles (these could be fridge magnets, foam letters, Scabble letters or printed letters – whatever you have to hand!)

Take a moment as a family to talk about some things that you are thankful for. Find the letters to make up the word for the things you want to say thanks to God for.

Talk about what you are thankful for with each other.

I wonder… what can we give thanks for?

Photocopying not permitted except under the CLA Church Licence.

8. Baptism candle

You will need: beeswax sheets cut into strips; candle wick cut to correct length

Take a piece of beeswax and wrap it very tightly around the candle wick. You can then use these candles for your prayer time during the celebration!

Talk about how a lit candle reminds us that Jesus, the light of the world, is always with us!

I wonder... what does the light of Jesus remind you of?

9. Baptism guessing game

You will need: numbered photos of people from your Messy Church being baptised (or as babies); guess the baby quiz form; pens

Set the photos of the babies up in your space and give each person a quiz sheet to record their guesses.

Talk about how sometimes people are baptised as babies, and sometimes as adults. Whenever someone is baptised, they are welcomed into Jesus' family. Can you guess who these members of Jesus' family are?

I wonder... who is in God's family?

10. Sensory play: Playdoh

You will need: Playdoh; craft tools (dough cutters in the shape of a cross, heart, dove, candle, etc. if you have them) and Playdoh mat (optional)

Create a sensory play station to allow free play and an opportunity to discuss the symbols involved in baptism at an age-appropriate level.

Talk about each of the symbols of baptism. What do they mean?

I wonder... why do you think these symbols of cross, heart, dove and candle were important to early Christians like Philip and the Ethiopian official?

Celebration

If you did the baptism guessing game in the activity time, you could use this as the introduction to your celebration as a way into the theme of 'A new direction' – God invites us all to become part of God's family through baptism.

If your team wants to focus on the social action idea, then you could include the demonstration described in that section. Wonder with the whole group how it feels to be those who have clean water and those who have unclean water. Who might be willing to help? What could the group do to make a change for those with unsafe or unclean water?

Sing a wonderful welcome song together.

Ask your gathered community how far they have travelled from home? Some will have been all over the world. Others may not have travelled outside their town or village or out of your state or nation.

In the days of the early church the followers of Jesus recalled him telling them to take the good news of God's love to their capital city (Jerusalem), then to their neighbouring country (Judea), then to people who were kind of seen as their enemies (Samaria) and then to the ends of the earth (Acts 1:8).

Ask the group if they know all the places where Messy Churches are?

Have a map or a list and pictures of Messy Churches in your city, region, state, nation and around the world to show on screen or printed out.

Messy Church all around the world is spreading the good news of Jesus.

Does anyone know how fast a horse and cart move when carrying passengers? Most historians agree that stagecoaches travelled about 8 kilometres or 5 miles an hour, which is twice as fast as most humans walk. Philip is running quite fast to keep up with the Ethiopians carriage, and he must have been fit too as he could also speak while he ran.

If you have time, you could see who the fastest runners in the group are?

The Dramatised Bible (edited by Michael Perry) provides excellent short scripts that you can copy and share to make the story come alive, that you can read aloud with some of your team 'miming' the actions or that you can retell in a 'godly play' style.

What is it about the story of God's love shown in Jesus that made the Ethiopian official want to be baptised there and then? Invite people to think about and share when they have taken a new direction or made a new start at something?

Invite people to share what they have made during the session time. See if they can share where or how their creative work helps them remember the story of Philip and the Ethiopian official.

You may like to have some information about what is involved in being baptised in your tradition available for people to read and/or talk about. If anyone is interested in being baptised, invite them to sit with your leader or clergy person over the meal or make an appointment at another time.

Wrap up with one or more of these wondering questions and then lead into prayers and share the Lord's Prayer together.

I wonder…
- When have you felt really close to God?
- When do you feel most part of God's worldwide family?
- How can we invite other people to be part of God's family?

Prayer
You could use the candles you made during the activity time and light them as each person prays, or use the words from the wondering words activity as a prompt for your community prayers.

Share your tradition's version of the Lord's Prayer together or search out some fresh expressions of the Lord's Prayer, e.g. the New Zealand Anglican Church has a rich cultural update of the prayer.

Song suggestions
'You are welcome' – Snack Music
'Celebrate' – Fischy Music
'Father welcomes' – Robin Mann (you may like to update the words with 'Our God welcomes all the children, we're one family through the Son', etc.)
'If you're black or if you're white or if you're in between, God loves you' – *Gospelling to the Beat*

Meal suggestions
Mallee quiche is an Aussie favourite that it easy to cook. It's sometimes called 'impossible quiche'. You can find a recipe online. Feel free to add whatever veggies are seasonal or grown in your garden! Eat with 'finger salad' (large cut-up veggie pieces that can be eaten with fingers).